OLD WORLD NEW

OLD WORLD NEW

FAMILY MEALS FROM THE HEART OF GENOA

LUCA MINNA & LAURA [illegible]

My Lady, who saw me laboring in deep suspense,
then said: "Heaven and all Nature
hangs from this pure spark of Divine light.

Look at the ring closest linked to this light,
and know that it moves so rapidly
because it is spurred onward by burning love."

La Donna mia, che mi vedea in cura
forte sospeso, disse: "Da quel punto
depende il Cielo e tutta la Natura.

Mira quel cerchio che più li è congiunto;
e sappi che 'l suo muovere è sì tosto
per l'affocato amore ond'elli è punto."

— Dante Alighieri, *Paradiso*

OLD WORLD NEW

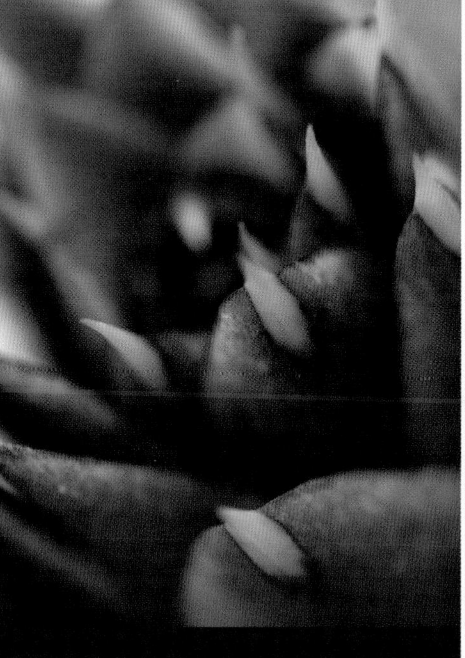

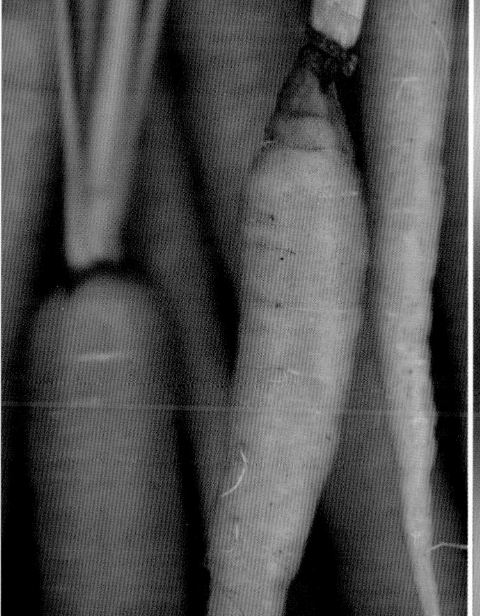

SPRING

SUMMER

FALL

WINTER

FARINA
FOCACCIA & CUCINA ITALIANA

ALL WE WANTED WAS A PLATE OF PESTO.

Some restaurants begin with a flash of inspiration. Ours arose from a series of disappointments.

It all started about seven years ago when we were sitting at a restaurant in New York, pondering the dish before us. The menu called it linguine with basil pesto, but the sauce was army green. The texture was chunky. The flavor was bitter. And the pasta was overcooked.

We'd ordered the dish in good faith, hoping it would taste like the pesto from our hometown of Genoa in north-western Italy. But it didn't. In fact, no matter where in America we traveled, and no matter which Italian restaurants we tried, we couldn't find pesto—or any other dish—that tasted like home.

Why not open our own restaurant?

We did. It's called FARINA. It opened five years ago in San Francisco, a city whose climate and culture resemble Genoa's—and whose agricultural bounty never fails.

Take the basil that we serve at FARINA. A local farmer grows it, harvests it by hand, and delivers it in his truck the very same morning. It actually looks and tastes like the basil grown in Genoa. The cooks at FARINA take that basil, coax it into pesto, and serve it over our signature mandilli di seta, *or silk handkerchief pasta.*

That pesto takes us home faster than any jet ever will.

While the basil in our pesto is important, the flour in our fresh pasta is critical. It's "tipo 00" from Molino Caputo in Naples, Italy. Its texture, its flavor, and its ethic inspire everything we do at FARINA. So much so, that we named the restaurant farina, *or flour. The name is more than a tribute to the finely ground wheat that is the cornerstone of our cuisine. It's also a daily reminder that our cooking and our own ethic must remain as pure and as humble as a mound of flour on a kitchen counter.*

Then again, that Caputo flour isn't all that humble. In each grain there lies the pride of an entire nation—a country in which food is a secular religion. At FARINA, we encourage this way of thinking. Every person who works here believes that a simple meal can surprise and delight, can nourish the soul as well as the body. It can even transport us.

FARINA is a labor of love, and this book is our firstborn. Please join us on our journey through the four seasons, from the fields to the markets to the kitchen—and from the old world of Italy to the new world of California. Then, near the end of the book, see twenty-six recipes arranged by season and presented as complete meals, from starter through dessert.

We hope you'll try these recipes. We hope you'll embrace their spirit and discover their magic. And whatever you do, when you're in San Francisco, please visit our restaurant. Sit down and relax with friends and family. Take the time to enjoy the flavors of Genoa, the flavors of home.

Luca Minna and Laura Garrone
Founders, FARINA

If you visit the Mission District in San Francisco and go to FARINA for dinner, do yourself a favor and scan the menu for a fish called branzino. If you find it, order it. When it arrives, do yourself another favor: Don't ask for a squeeze of lemon to go with it. If you do, the chef will send a few lemon wedges to your table, but inside, he'll be seething. *"Volete spremere del limone sul mio branzino? Mah, cose te dixi, belinun?!!"**

To Paolo Laboa, the founding chef at FARINA, a squeeze of lemon is an insult felt halfway around the world. That's because if you splash acid on the branzino, you don't just insult Paolo. You insult his uncle, who fished the waters off Genoa for forty years. You insult his grandmother, who reserved cooking vessels exclusively for fish, because over time those vessels acquired and imparted a subtle, briny essence. And you insult the branzino itself, because as an Italian fish, it has strict ideas on how it should be cooked and served.

And the offenses don't end with a squeeze of lemon.

If you mistake a truffle for a mushroom, you insult the forager who taught a young Paolo how to hunt for truffles in the forests north of Genoa. If you salt your focaccia, you insult the baker who sprayed the dough with salted water, added a few crystals of coarse sea salt, and then sprinkled the dough with olive oil, trapping the crystals beneath each drop of oil and leaving a vapor trail of salt, in just the right amount. If you suggest that Paolo add parsley to his basil pesto, you insult the chefs in the Genoa restaurants where Paolo learned his way. You insult the farmer who grows the basil whose curved leaves and subtle flavor take Paolo straight back to his mother's kitchen. And you insult Paolo himself whose recipe, in 2008, won the Pesto World Championship in Genoa.

Above all, you insult the ingredients. Please don't.

Paolo says that ingredients have feelings. You don't yell "Bam!" at them. You don't turn them into foam or wrap them in plastic and cook them in warm water. You don't call them "slow" or "artisan" or "authentic" or any other word that smells of fashion. Instead, you coddle them. You honor them with traditional preparations; you add a twist here and there to keep them fresh; you fine-tune their proportions to suit the weather and the season and the time of day. You even sing to them. That's what Paolo does. His mother did, too. We are not making this up.

*"You want to squeeze lemon on my branzino? What are you talking about, d***head?"

In the end, FARINA is about respect. It's about shaving just the right amount of white truffle over a plate of taglierini. It's about creating a new menu each morning to showcase fresh local ingredients that the chefs, in their weaker moments, will admit rival the best of Italy. It's about a chef, late each evening, serving "family meal" to his staff at the large center table in the restaurant dining room, among the guests. Above all, it's a celebration of simple, honest dishes, prepared and served with all the love that the best home cooks still lavish on their families.

This book, then, is a love song to a vanishing way of cooking and way of life that survives and even thrives at FARINA, kept alive by chefs—Paolo, Angelo, Davide—who are so "Italian" that they're almost caricatures, and so retro that they might be radical.

Paolo Laboa
Executive Chef

While Paolo Laboa grew up in Genoa and learned his trade in the kitchens of Genovese masters, chef Angelo Auriana, from Bergamo, and chef Davide Cogliati, from Milan, contribute fresh perspectives and approaches. They help to make FARINA a multi-regional mosaic and a source of ever-evolving *cucina italiana.*

SPRING

FOCACCINA GENOVESE CON PROSCIUTTO DI PARMA E BURRATA

Focaccia is to Genoa as the baguette is to Paris, and many of the best Italian cooks wouldn't dream of trusting this staple to an outside bakery. Paolo, for instance, makes his own *focaccina* every day, as his mother did, and her mother before her. He mixes the dough, waits for the rise, shapes the loaves by hand, and fries each loaf in olive oil to give the crust its signature savor and gentle crunch. Some days, Paolo adds potatoes to the dough; other times he folds cheese into the mix. He tops each focaccina with burrata cheese and prosciutto di Parma, the raw-cured ham that is nutty, fragrant, and so tender it almost melts. You can serve this dish as a starter, as lunch, or as a light supper.

For recipe, see page 151.

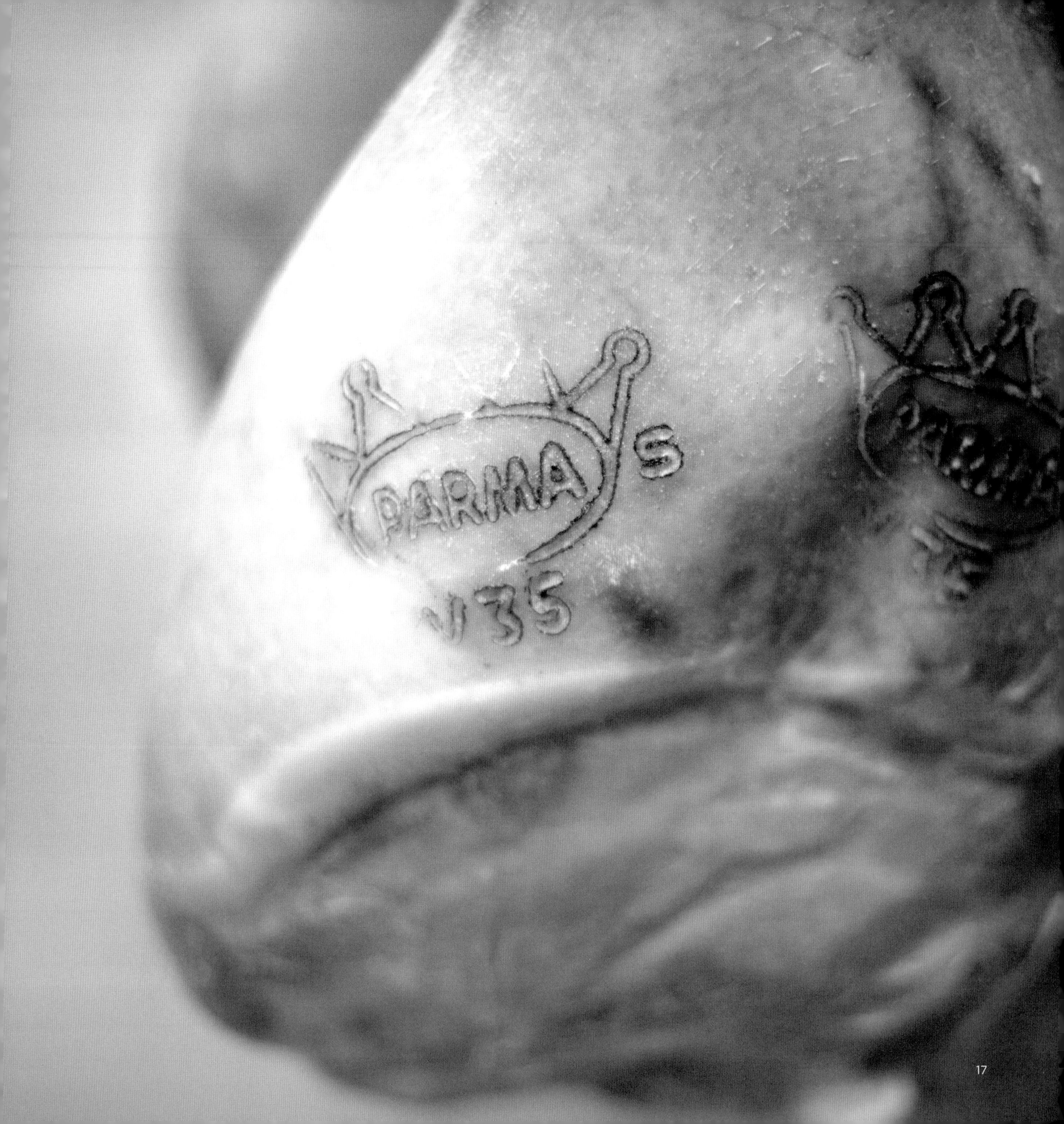
PARMA
S
V35

LEFT: As hams hang in this aging room, fermentation works its magic. RIGHT: Formed into pouches and filled with fresh cream, mozzarella becomes burrata, which means "buttered" in Italian. Try it once and you'll see why burrata inspires cheese lovers worldwide. FAR RIGHT: Balls of focaccina dough receive a quick dusting of flour before being shaped and then fried in olive oil.

LEFT AND ABOVE: Taste the marriage of prosciutto and burrata, sweet and savory, cracked pepper and olive oil. You could say that this topping elevates the focaccina. Then again, bread this good is already exalted. RIGHT: While white wine is a common companion to prosciutto di Parma, red can also work well with focaccina. Keep it on the light side: think Dolcetto di Dogliani by Chionetti or Schiava by Elena Walch.

PANE AL ROSMARINO

In Italy, where homemade bread is a mark of family identity, Paolo learned early the challenges and rewards of bringing flour to life with water and yeast. Each morning his house grew warm with the smells of baking dough as his mother prepared enough bread to last the day. Proper welcoming of guests, Paolo discovered, included a basket of bread and a bowl of cured olives. Today, Paolo maintains this personal approach to bread. Late each evening, he and his staff leave their dough to rise, and by midmorning the restaurant kitchen is filled with fragrance and warmth as loaves grow hot in the ovens. Many days, Paolo follows a trick used by his mother and rolls the dough in nuts or fresh herbs. The rosemary adds a piney note to the morning air at FARINA.

For recipe, see page 151.

ABOVE: Coarsely ground by Molino Caputo in Naples, Italy, this wheat approaches its destiny as flour. RIGHT: Shaped and separated, the loaves are left to rise a second time. They assume their basic shape and then bake in the oven where, 25 minutes later, they emerge as the cornerstone of a good meal—and an edible symbol of the FARINA philosophy.

CAPPELLACCI DI MELANZANE E ZUCCHINI AL BURRO E TIMO

While they have the same name as Italian dumplings that are most often filled with winter squash, these particular *cappellacci* are a warm-weather specialty unique to Paolo's family. His mother first created the recipe many years ago when, feeling overwhelmed by a bumper crop of zucchini and eggplant, she created the puffy disks of dough that resemble the skull caps worn by Roman Catholic cardinals. The dish became a family favorite and Paolo took it with him when he started cooking professionally. Each element serves a distinct purpose, says Paolo. The marjoram adds floral and citrus notes while the eggplant's faint bitterness balances the zucchini's mild sweetness. And the Brie? It's both bitter and sweet, a miracle of fermentation, and proof that even proud Genovese cooks will reach across the border for the right ingredient.

For recipe, see page 152.

LEFT: Razor-sharp steel turns garlic cloves into a pungent mince. BELOW: Hand-mixed dough of flour, egg, wine, and cheese will soon be turned into pasta. RIGHT: Each spoonful of filling, atop a thin sheet of pasta, awaits its lid.

LEFT: Another sheet of pasta is laid on top and gently pressed around each dollop of filling, producing a strip of pasta pillows. RIGHT: Quick work with a cookie cutter liberates the cappellacci one at a time. BELOW: Gentle crimping seals in the mixture of eggplant, zucchini, and cheese.

A fresh white wine with herbal notes, such as the Langhe Anas-Cetta by Elvio Cogno, makes a fine match for cappellacci. LEFT: Fresh-grated cheese, a drizzle of browned butter, and a sprig of thyme complete the dish.

TAGLIATA DI TONNO CON ASPARAGI, SPUMA DI BURRATA, E RIDUZIONE D'AGLIANICO

While Paolo grew up cooking and eating bonito, one of the most common tunas in the Gulf of Genoa, he would later discover the much larger yellowfin tuna caught in the waters off southern Italy. Today, Paolo prefers the yellowfin's brilliant red slabs. Marinated with oregano and basil and juniper berries, this fish matches well with fresh produce from the hills of Liguria—and from the valleys of California. A mainstay of FARINA's springtime menu combines yellowfin tuna with asparagus and burrata cheese. Alive with coastal flavors and the scent of the sea, it's the next best thing to an evening in Genoa.

For recipe, see page 153.

ABOVE LEFT: Morning at the market in Genoa. Savvy buyers arrive early and pay top euro for the best fish. LEFT: On the marble counter at FARINA, a slab of yellowfin tuna gives way at the touch of a knife. RIGHT: To get the sweetest asparagus, shop early in the season and choose the smaller, thinner stalks. Then, to preserve their color and character, blanch them in salted water and cool them before you sauté them in olive oil.

A crisp Italian *rosato* such as Salice Salentino by Villa Mottura, halfway between red and white, works well with an aquatic meat that stands halfway between pork and beef.

Seared on the outside, rare on the inside, and served with soft burrata cheese, sautéed asparagus, and dots of red wine reduction: this may be tuna's highest expression.

CIME DI PISELLI SALTATI ALL'OLIO D'OLIVA

Deprivation can be delicious. Take pea tendrils. These leaves, strings, and stems aren't really meant to be food; they're mere cuttings, snipped in springtime to tame unruly pea vines. But then some Genovese gardener, most likely in a time of need, had the presence of mind to gather these greens and cook them up. Sautéed in olive oil with salt and red pepper flakes, they prove, once again, that a good cook can make the most of a "lowly" ingredient, and that simple can be sublime.

For recipe, see page 154.

If basil pesto is Genoa's gift to the world, oranges are one of the world's gifts to Genoa. There, bathed in sunshine and sheltered from north winds by the Apennines, they grow sweet and fragrant but retain just enough zing to cut through the fat of rich treats such as *latte dolce fritto,* or sweet milk fritters. The fritters themselves are bite-sized blocks of delicious, enriched with cinnamon and vanilla. Long ago, these two exotics entailed months of arduous travel. No wonder Christopher Columbus, merchant captain and native son of Genoa, sailed westward in search of a faster spice route to Asia.

For recipe, see page 154.

LEFT: With their crunchy sweet tartness, candied oranges make a wonderful companion to sweet milk fritters. To make the oranges, start with a simple syrup (one part water and one part sugar, stirred at a simmer until sugar dissolves, and then cooled). Then take an orange or two and slice thinly. Place the slices on a rack and brush them liberally with syrup, on both sides. Dry the slices in an oven at 250°F until "they're like potato chips," says Paolo.

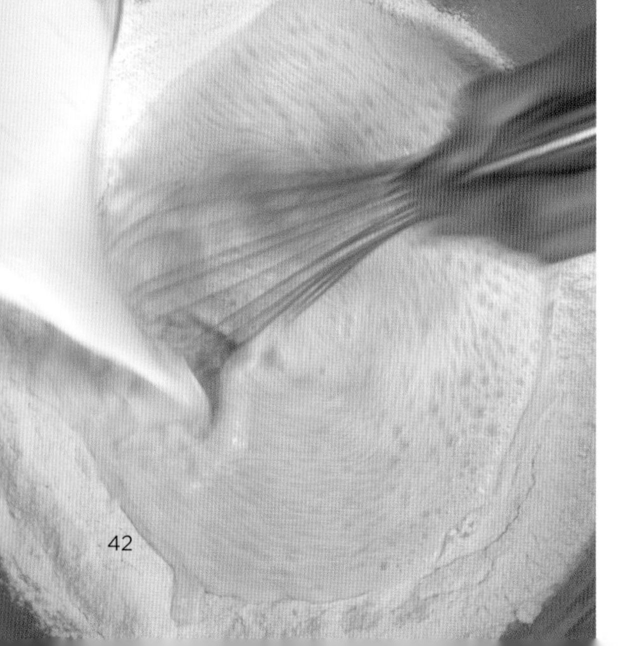

ABOVE LEFT: When you zest the orange, go easy with the peeler or paring knife. You want to keep the blade shallow so that you pick up only the outer peel and leave the bitter white pith behind. If, after peeling, you spot any remaining pith, lay the peel flat on a cutting board, orange side down, and slice away the white stuff.

ABOVE LEFT: Steady whisking creates a smooth and luscious custard. Once you cut it into squares, you dust it with flour, dip it in egg, roll it in bread crumbs, and fry it in a pan. A quick dip in a plate of sugar completes the transformation.

For many people from Liguria, a dessert of cappuccino and latte dolce fritto isn't just a treat; it's a birthright. Wherever you live, or wherever you're from, do as the Italians do: Eat some fritter. Nibble an orange. Sip some froth. Repeat.

SUMMER

CAPESANTE ROSTICCIATE CON COLINO DI POMODORI E OLIO AL BASILICO

In early summer when basil season begins, Genovese cooks celebrate with their own twist on surf and turf. They start with their local basil, so fragrant that just one whiff can stop farmers' market shoppers in their tracks. Then they add sun-soaked tomatoes from Campania, and *capesante,* or scallops, plucked from the Gulf of Genoa by "day boats" that return to the docks early each afternoon to ensure the freshest catch. These three main ingredients create an edible ode to sun, soil, and sea.

For recipe, see page 155.

ABOVE: Sliced cleanly in half, drizzled with olive oil, and seasoned with thyme and salt, these tomatoes roast until soft and smoky. RIGHT: Use only the freshest scallops: firm, moist, and translucent. FARTHER RIGHT: Olive oil, infused with the essence of basil, tastes of summer. FARTHEST RIGHT: Roasted tomatoes surrender their juices to gravity.

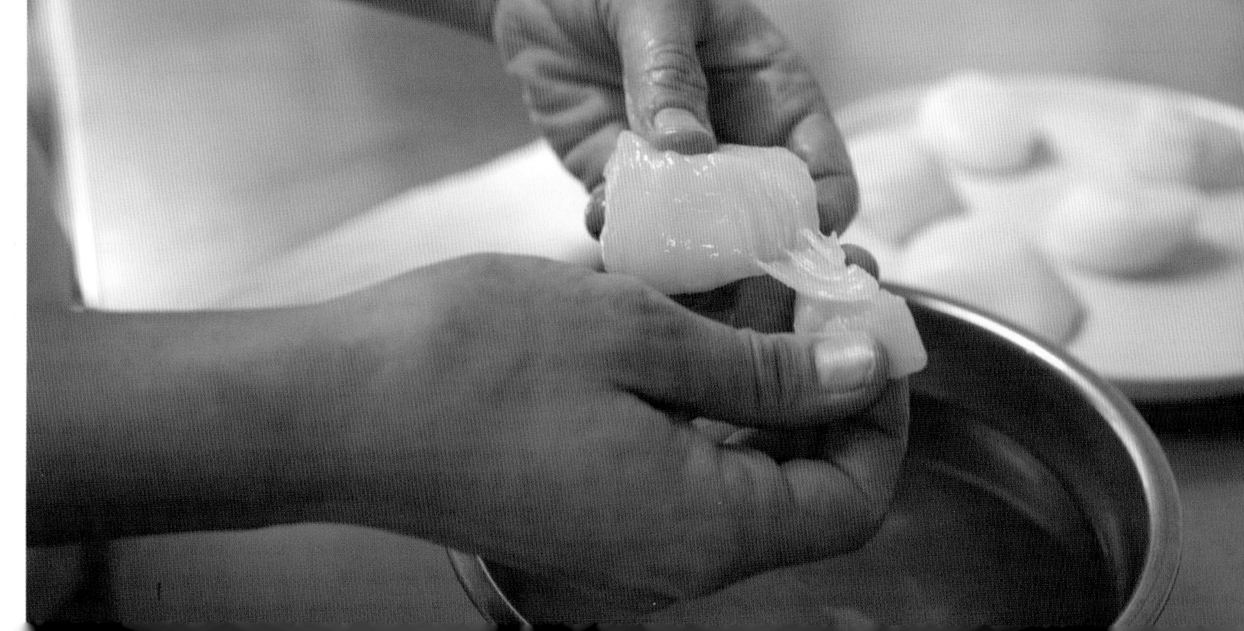

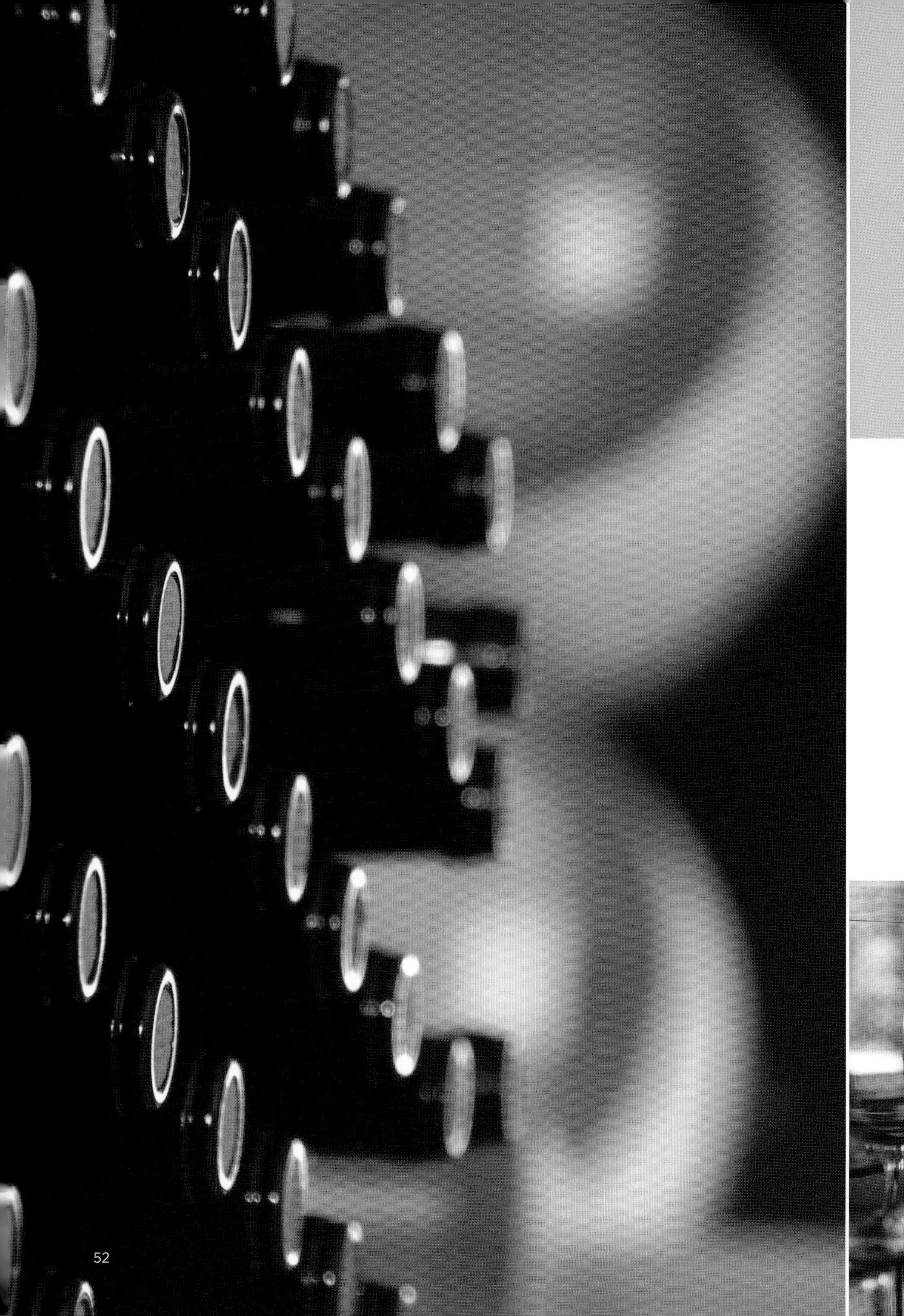

LEFT: At once rich and subtle, scallops want a wine that is both flinty and fruity. Try a Gavi di Gavi Black Label by La Scolca in Piedmont. RIGHT: Seared until golden brown and served three to a plate, these tender medallions make a beautiful beginning to a meal.

PANE CON OLIVE TAGGIASCHE

To many people in Genoa, it's a sin to serve bread without olives alongside. Most folks prefer the *taggiasca* olive, a local favorite that, when pressed, produces an oil milder and more refined than Tuscan blends. Fresh taggiasche are also soaked in water for forty days and then cured in brine scented with thyme, rosemary, and bay laurel. When the cure is complete, these olives soon find their way into all kinds of salads and main courses. Paolo's mother often folded them into her bread dough. Today, the cooks at FARINA do the same.

For recipe, see page 156.

ABOVE: After a long soak in herb-scented brine, these taggiasche olives await their moment in the oven or on the table. RIGHT: With practice, you can create bread loaves of uniform shape and size. Then again, minor variations add a rustic charm.

MANDILLI DI SETA AL PESTO GENOVESE

Paolo grew up on *Ocimum basilicum 'Genovese.'* Most Genovese children do. They smell it in the farmers' markets, trample it in kitchen gardens, and taste it fresh and in pesto. By the time they can walk, most can't live without the trademark flavor of their native basil. And if, when they grow up, their dreams carry them far from Italy, most abandon hope of finding true Genovese basil in their new towns and cities. So imagine Paolo's surprise when he, on a quick trip to a San Francisco supermarket to buy laundry detergent, caught a familiar scent wafting from the next aisle. There, behind a display of cut flowers and potted herbs, he found Genovese basil. This is the herb so prized in Genoa that it's protected by a guarantee of authenticity called *Denominazione di Origine Protetta* (Protected Designation of Origin). Paolo sniffed. He bought. He called the farmer whose name was stuck to the plastic pot. After a trip to the farm and a talk with the farmer, Paolo secured his source for the basil of his childhood.

For recipe, see page 157.

ABOVE: Nuts of the Italian stone pine are vital to the flavor of basil pesto. The *pignolia* differ markedly from Asian pine nuts, containing less oil and more flavors of earth and pine. RIGHT: To make FARINA's signature dish, start with *Ocimum basilicum 'Genovese,'* pluck the best leaves from each stem, and then soak the leaves in water to soften their flavor.

THE PESTO OF CHAMPIONS

When Paolo learned the art of pesto from his mother, he never thought of entering the old family recipe in any competition. But in 2008, when the annual Pesto World Championship gave him a chance to fly home to Genoa, he decided to go for it. There, at the Palazzo Ducale in Genoa's old town, a jury of trained tasters declared Paolo's pesto the best in the world. All 100 finalists from near and far used the very same ingredients, so proportions and *un certo non so che* (a certain something) made all the difference. Today, this very pesto is available in a jar, with its texture and savor intact. So if you don't have time to make the recipe on page 157, you can still taste championship flavor.

LEFT: After thirty years in the kitchen, Paolo eyeballs everything and cooks by intuition. Just the same, we recommend that you closely follow the measurements in his recipe for pesto—at least the first few times you make it. ABOVE: Paolo's pesto is unusually light and creamy. RIGHT: A splash of pasta water melts the cheese and gently warms the pesto.

LEFT: *Doppio zero* flour for pasta is relatively low in gluten, so it creates tender noodles. Eggs add flavor, body, and protein. RIGHT: White wine fills the role of water and imparts a sweet smoothness. BELOW: *Mandilli di seta,* or silk handkerchiefs, create a beautiful platform for pesto. FAR RIGHT: Repeated runs through the pasta machine produce long, soft sheets that shimmer like polished cotton.

The finished mandilli, bathed in creamy pesto and draped in silken folds, is a signature dish, unique to FARINA. Paolo likes to serve it with a crisp Ligurian Pigato by Piero Lugano.

DENTICE IN BRODETTO CON CARCIOFI

Paolo's uncle was a fisherman in Genoa. On Sundays, in his shack strewn with nets and tackle, the uncle would serve whole *dentice rosso,* a local Thai snapper. He also kept the heads, bones, and skins of filleted fish and simmered them into a fragrant broth to which he added carrots, celery, onion, herbs, white wine, and crushed tomatoes. He drizzled this *brodetto,* or "little broth," over the roasted fish, heightening its flavor and fragrance. Today, dentice with broth and artichokes is a customer favorite whenever it appears on FARINA's summertime menu.

For recipe, see page 158.

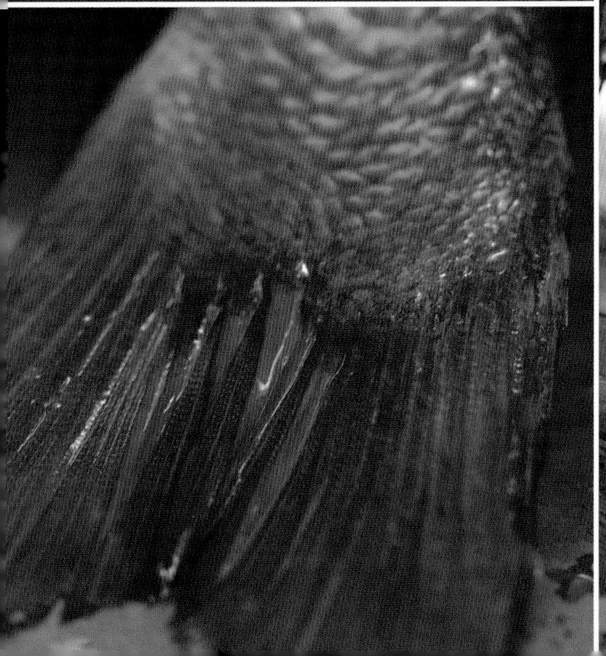

TOP LEFT: A permanent squint tells the story of a fisherman's life on the water. LEFT: These Thai snapper are so fresh they're almost flopping. Out of the oven, they receive a finishing splash of olive oil.

The snapper sizzles outside while its moist, steaming flesh awaits the fork. LEFT: With this fish, try the white Ligurian wine called Cinque Terre from the Cooperativa Agricoltura di Riomaggiore. Made from grapes grown on terraces carved out of sea cliffs, it has an oceanic tang.

MELANZANE ALLA PARMIGIANA

When life gives you eggplants, bake them in a casserole. That's the idea behind eggplant parmesan. This dish, born in southern Italy around 1800, made the most of the dark purple fruits that sprang in abundance from every home garden, and of the tomatoes that were just catching on in the Old World. Home cooks sliced their eggplants, pan-fried them, and layered them along with tomato sauce, basil, and cheese. The resulting dish resembled lasagna, but without the meat and flour and eggs that could be scarce and expensive. Soon *melanzane alla parmigiana* made its way north to Genoa, where Paolo's forebears adopted and adapted it. Today, this dish is a classic—and another case of necessity made delicious.

For recipe, see page 159.

LEFT: San Marzano tomatoes, grown in the volcanic soil near Mount Vesuvius, make famously flavorful sauce—just right for this dish. Basil leaves add a fresh herbal note.

CESTINO DI PASTA MATTA CON FRAGOLE

All over northwestern Italy, food lovers hunt the hills for wild *fragole,* or strawberries. They're so delicious that most are eaten on the spot, but a few make it to market, where Paolo snapped them up during his days in Genoa. In California, he looks to the farms of the Salinas Valley for the best strawberries. Placed atop his *cestino,* a dessert of traditional Italian components combined in a personal creation, the bright, sweet berries complement the cool cream filling and the crisp tuile basket that contains it.

For recipe, see page 160.

BELOW: Tuile batter (no one is sure how it came to be called *pasta matta,* or crazy dough) of flour, butter, egg whites, and sugar is spread over a baking sheet. Baked until it's golden tan on the edges, this disk is, for about thirty seconds, flexible enough to mold into a basket shape. BELOW LEFT: Mixed with water and carefully heated, sugar caramelizes and turns into a thick syrup that can be spun into a golden spiral.

LEFT: Vigorous whisking quickly doubles the volume of the cream filling. ABOVE: The cooled filling, fragrant with Grand Marnier and luscious with mascarpone cheese, is ready for spooning into tuile baskets.

Coils of caramelized sugar add edible beauty to dessert. RIGHT: Rich yet refreshing, cestino makes a wonderful ending to a summer meal and a fine vehicle for the season's best strawberries.

FALL

CALAMARI AL PIGATO CON PATATA SCHIACCIATA ALLO ZAFFERANO

When dinner swims into the Ligurian Sea, the fleets of Genoa answer. Fishermen in skiffs, long practiced in the pursuit, drape purse seines around the dense schools of fish and squid, fill their holds, and return to the docks to a warm response from local seafood fans. For weeks until the squid depart for deep water, heaps of fried calamari appear on platters all over the city. The delicate meat of the squid also cooks quickly on a hot skillet; it inspired Paolo's *calamari al Pigato,* now a seasonal starter at FARINA. Paolo sautés the squid with garlic, chili flakes, and salt, then adds a cup of Pigato wine that mingles with the pan juices to create a light and mouthwatering sauce.

For recipe, see page 161.

ABOVE: The Genoa shoreline is blessed with scenic bays and inlets, such as this fisherman's cove at Boccadasse. They make the fishing life look romantic, but spend a day in this skiff, on the pitch and roll of the Ligurian Sea, hauling sodden nets, and you'll never again question the price of your seafood.

RIGHT: When shopping for squid, follow the same guidelines you would use for finfish: clear eyes, shiny skin, and an ocean smell that's not fishy. BELOW: Calamari cooks quickly. Keep it moving. As soon as the pan juices turn opaque and the squid turns a pale brown, it's ready.

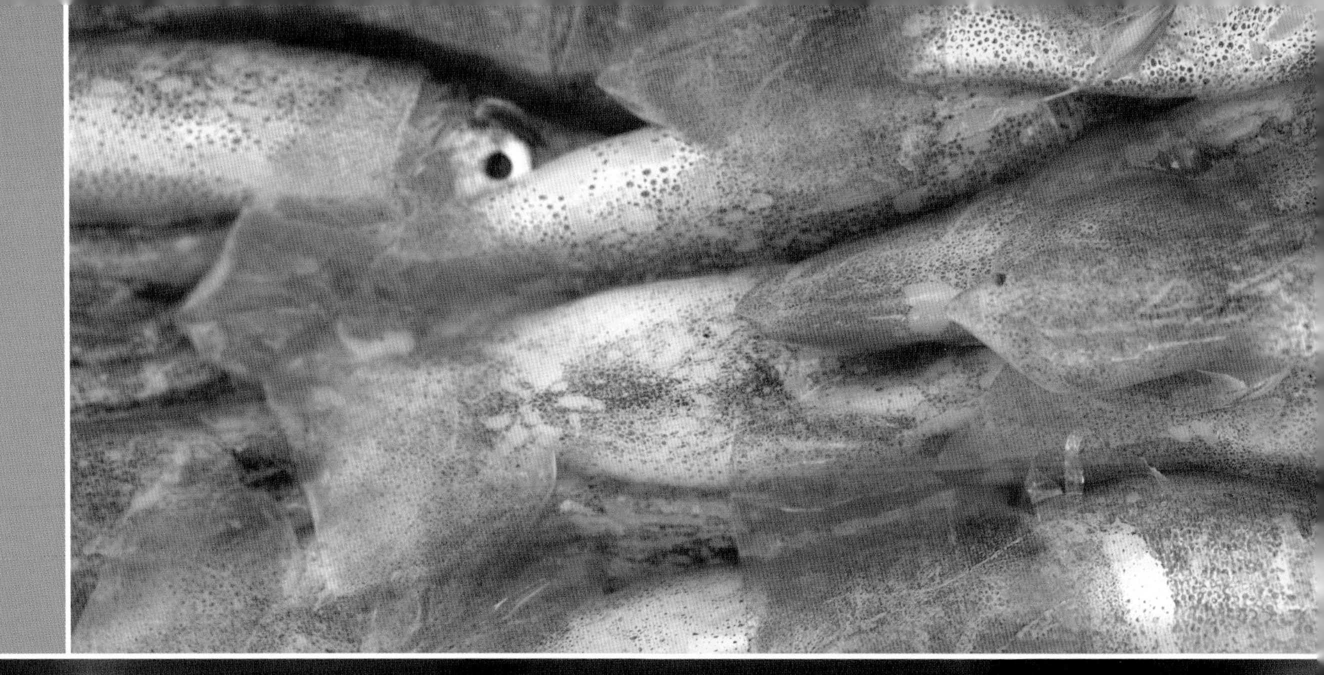

ABOVE: True to its Chardonnay fruit, this Gaia & Rey wine from Piedmont is rich and slightly buttery. True to its Italian origin, it's also fresh and food-friendly. RIGHT: Pan-fried calamari over saffron mashed potatoes: a dish conceived by peasants, fit for a king.

PANE DI PATATE

It's been 400 years since the Genovese thought of potatoes as poison from Peru. Today, Paolo uses them often—even in his bread dough. When mashed, they add body, mild flavor, and starch that retains moisture and creates a soft, smooth texture. Sometimes Paolo adds mashed, starchy potatoes to the dough as usual, and then, during the second rise, he slices off the top of the dough, adds a layer of potato slices and a few sage leaves, and replaces the top. The slices add a chewy, savory surprise.

For recipe, see page 162.

ABOVE: Before the first rise, Paolo sprinkles the dough with olive oil for extra flavor and moisture. He prefers a slightly wet dough because it creates chewier bread. RIGHT: During the second rise, he adds potato slices and sage leaves—a classic combination of earthy and herbal flavors.

PAPPARDELLE AL ROSMARINO CON FUNGHI PORCINI

The word *porcini* inspires a Pavlovian response in mushroom lovers everywhere—and in mushroom foragers all over northern Italy and northern California. The foragers hike for miles in search of the plump brown caps, nestled among pine needles or fallen chestnut leaves. No other mushroom offers the meaty texture and nutty flavor of the "little piglet," and no other has its culinary range, from stews to sauces to simple slices, grilled or lightly sautéed. In this dish, Paolo cooks porcini slices in olive oil with garlic and parsley, and then serves them over fresh pappardelle noodles, rich with egg and fragrant with rosemary.

For recipe, see page 163.

The sign of healthy porcini? Pale stalks and proud brown caps with no black spots or yellow-brown shading on the underside.

FAR LEFT: Plump, broad rosemary leaves contribute soft, round flavors. LEFT: The prized porcini, sliced and ready. BELOW: Make your pasta about the thickness of lasagna noodles. Dust it with flour before you cut it so the ribbons won't stick together while they wait to be cooked.

This simple pasta dish calls for a wine that won't overpower it. Try a Casot dan Vian—little house in the vineyard—a Piedmontese white by Scagliola that's somehow crisp and round at the same time.

TENERO D'AGNELLO LARDELLATO AL TARTUFO NERO

It looks like a dirt clod and smells like mold. So what makes the black truffle so coveted by food-savvy sophisticates from Genoa to Tokyo? Mostly it's the scent: earthy, musky, pungent. Partly it's the flavor: an umami blast from a primordial past. But it's also the romance of the primitive. The truffle is, after all, a wrinkled brown parasite that feeds off a tree root. It's a wild, foraged tuber that refuses to be cultivated. It's hunted in deep woods by dogs, pigs, and poachers; dug from damp earth beneath blankets of leaves; sold from the trunks of cars after dark. It's mystery and magic. It's rare by nature. It's the diamond of the kitchen. And in the hands of a chef like Paolo, it's edible art.

For recipe, see page 164.

ABOVE: Lamb has a wild side, as do black truffles. It's only fitting that they meet in Paolo's kitchen and mingle with bay leaves, juniper berries, and other untamed flavors. ABOVE RIGHT: This lamb loin, cut from the rack and filled with a mixture of black truffles, marjoram, pancetta, and olive oil, needs only a dusting of flour and a roll in a fry pan. RIGHT: Paolo throws in a few sage leaves to add another layer of flavor.

PRODUTTORI del BARBARESCO
CN/501

LEFT: What to drink with lamb loins stuffed with black truffles and Italian bacon? Barbaresco from the Cantina Sociale dei Produttori. This red wine from the truffle country of Piedmont tastes of cherry, fennel, and licorice—good with the gently gamy flavors on the plate. ABOVE: Made with wine, plum tomatoes, and nine aromatics, this complex, slow-simmered sauce is far more than a garnish.

BROCCOLINI

If you ask Paolo to share the inspiration behind his broccolini side dish, he shrugs. "It's broccolini," he says. "Simple." He has a point. This cross between broccoli and Chinese broccoli is best prepared in a straightforward manner. Just blanch it in salted water and then sauté it in olive oil with garlic, a pinch of red chili flakes, and a sprinkle of salt. The sweet, tender stems and florets are so delicious that most people want a plateful, solo. But broccolini makes a fine companion, too. At FARINA, Paolo serves it with lamb.

For recipe, see page 165.

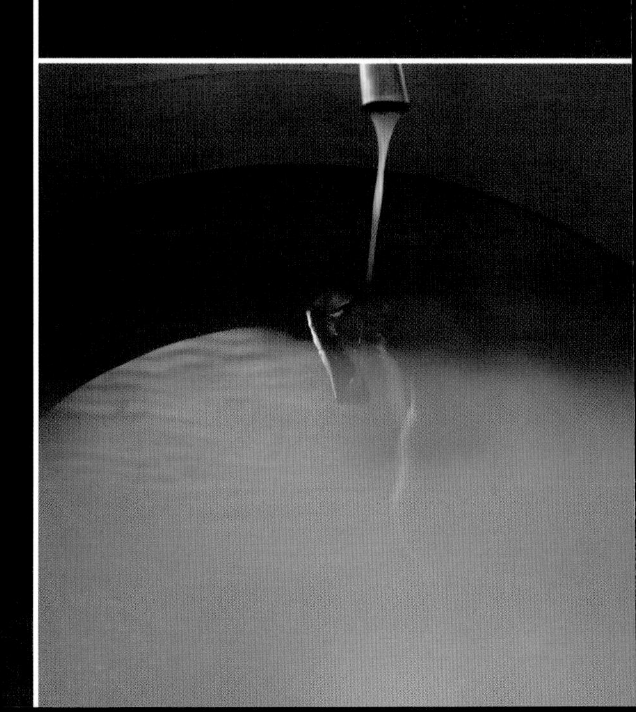

SACRIPANTINA

In Genoa, the *sacripantina* cake is popular at weddings, birthdays, baptisms, and other celebrations. At FARINA, it's a celebration in itself when Paolo puts it on the menu. For one thing, this sponge cake takes an unusual shape: it's a golden dome that's sprung from a bowl. For another, Paolo makes his version with three layers of buttercream—vanilla, chocolate, and hazelnut—that add tantalizing flavor to each bite. And for all its buttery richness, this cake tastes so light, you'll have room for a second slice.

For recipe, see page 166.

To make a memory, you have to break some eggs. LEFT: The first layer of cake awaits the scented slather of vanilla buttercream.

ABOVE: The initial light whisking can be done by hand, but for the heavy lifting, you'll want to switch to a stand mixer. RIGHT: Gentle folding keeps the batter light and airy. FAR RIGHT TOP: Resist the temptation to set out these bowls of buttercream and call them dessert. FAR RIGHT BOTTOM: Each layer of buttercream supports the next layer of cake.

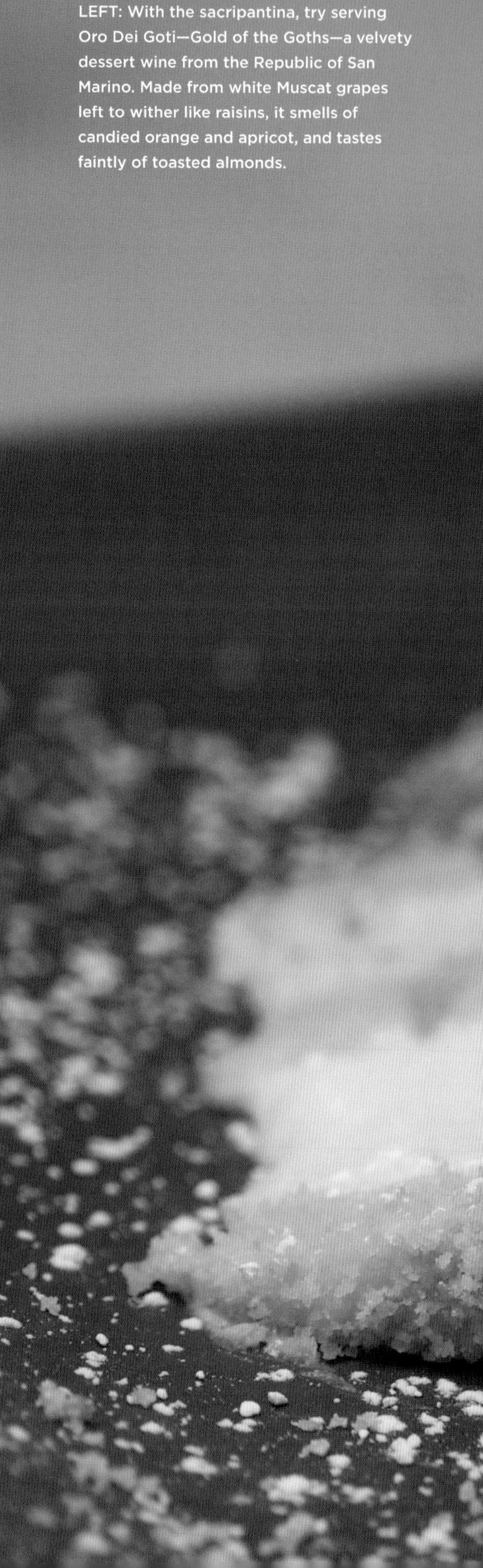

LEFT: With the sacripantina, try serving Oro Dei Goti—Gold of the Goths—a velvety dessert wine from the Republic of San Marino. Made from white Muscat grapes left to wither like raisins, it smells of candied orange and apricot, and tastes faintly of toasted almonds.

WINTER

TORTINO DI CARCIOFI

While it arose in North Africa and spread to Sicily, many Genovese cooks argue that the artichoke thrives best in Liguria. Here, in the mild maritime climate, *carciofi* remain tender. And inside each thistle, beyond the thorny leaves and the fibrous choke, beats a heart of pure flavor. In Genoa, cooks take artichokes and boil them, bake them, fry them, grill them, stuff them, build risotto dishes around them. Paolo? He does all of these things, but in these pages he bakes a type of frittata called a *tortino.* It's a light, savory start to a winter meal.

For recipe, see page 167.

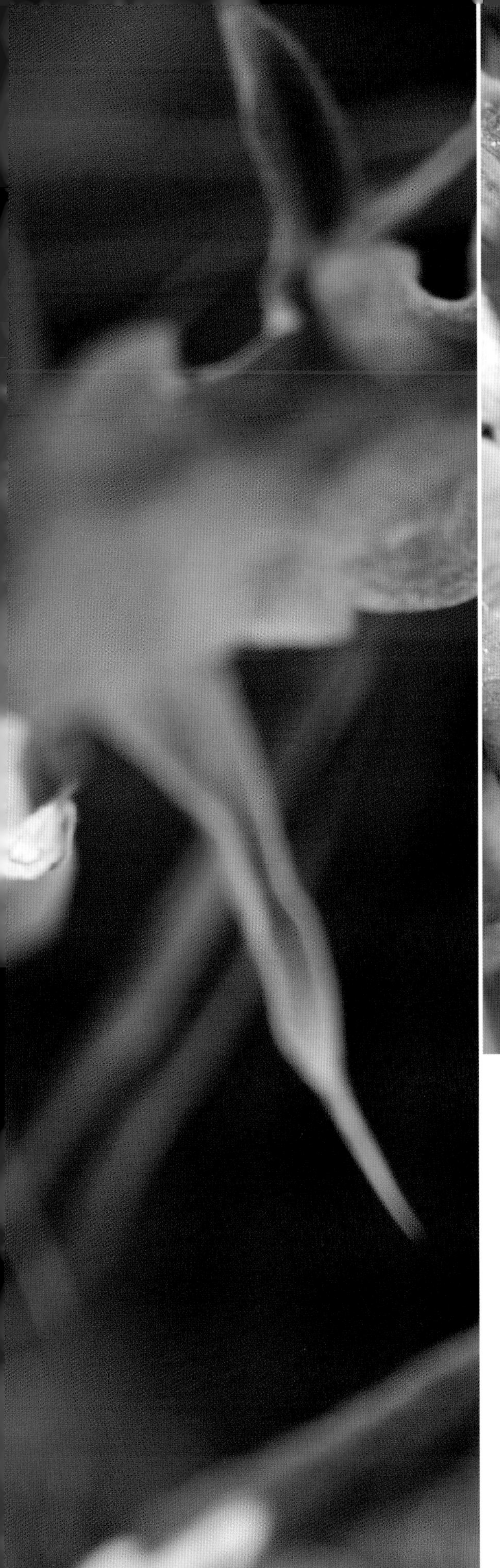

LEFT: The *violetto,* the celebrated purple artichoke of northern Italy, produces a spiked lavender flower that resembles a sea urchin. But long before it blooms, this gargantuan flower bud produces wonderful flavors. When shopping for artichokes of whatever color, look for heavy ones with firm stems and tightly bundled leaves.

ABOVE LEFT: If you find fresh artichokes with the stems still on, get them. The stems are a smooth, sweet extension of the heart, so slice them up and enjoy them. RIGHT: Paolo doesn't get nervous when preparing delicate frittatas and soufflés. Thirty years of practice lends him palpable confidence in the kitchen.

Because artichokes and wine don't mix well, you might want to skip wine during your tortino course. But if you insist, pour a Vermentino Colli di Luni. Made from grapes grown on the border of Liguria and Tuscany, it's a natural peacemaker.

PANE DI CASTAGNE CON NOCI

Many Ligurians owe their existence to chestnuts. Way back before the potato emigrated to the Old World, the smooth brown *castagne,* harvested in late autumn, provided starch and sustenance for people struggling to farm the tiny strips of arable land between the sea and the mountains. In some winters, they ate little else. Today, chestnuts remain a staple. They're boiled, roasted, and ground into flour. They're used in pastas, gnocchi, sweets—and bread. In winter, Paolo adds chestnut flour to his bread dough to lend it rustic warmth and savor.

For recipe, see page 168.

Walnuts have nearly as many calories as butter and almost as much protein as steak, so they're a good foil for low-fat, carbohydrate-rich chestnuts.

FAR LEFT: Wheat flour, being light and airy, is God's gift to bread bakers. Chestnut flour, about as light as a boat anchor, can be a curse. So when making his chestnut bread with walnuts, Paolo uses an eleven-to-one ratio of wheat to chestnut.

The second rise begins. At this stage, the yeast keeps feeding on flour and water, turning starches into sugars and producing carbon dioxide bubbles that give the bread its structure and lift. The dough also develops a “skin” that preserves the loaf’s shape as it expands.

TAGLIERINI AI VENTI ROSSI CON TRIFOLA BIANCA

When Paolo was a teenager in Genoa, eager to hunt truffles with the local experts, they agreed to take him along on one condition: that he drink a lot on the way to prime truffle territory. He agreed. The next morning, he found a small bag of white truffles on his kitchen table, but he couldn't remember where, or even if, he had found them. That's the way it is in truffle country, where the best spots are kept secret and where a well-trained, truffle-sniffing dog is a prized companion. From early October through the end of January, our forager, Antonino Marchelli, and other truffle seekers sift the leaves beneath oak, willow, poplar, and linden trees in search of the *tartufi* whose musky aroma tantalizes eaters everywhere—and whose market price turns this annual harvest into a treasure hunt.

For recipe, see page 169.

Truffles are famously aromatic, but they're hard to find because they grow a few inches beneath the soil's surface. That's why dogs, with their sensitive noses, are so important to the hunt. (Some locals claim that mongrels make the best truffle finders, because purebred dogs can't smell as well. As for trained pigs, few truffle foragers use them any more. A pig that finds a truffle won't budge.)

Fresh truffles deserve the freshest eggs possible—preferably laid by pasture-raised hens whose diets create rich, flavorful yolks. LEFT: At a price north of $3,000 a pound, these *trifola bianca* are precious cargo. Fortunately, just a few shavings impart powerful flavor.

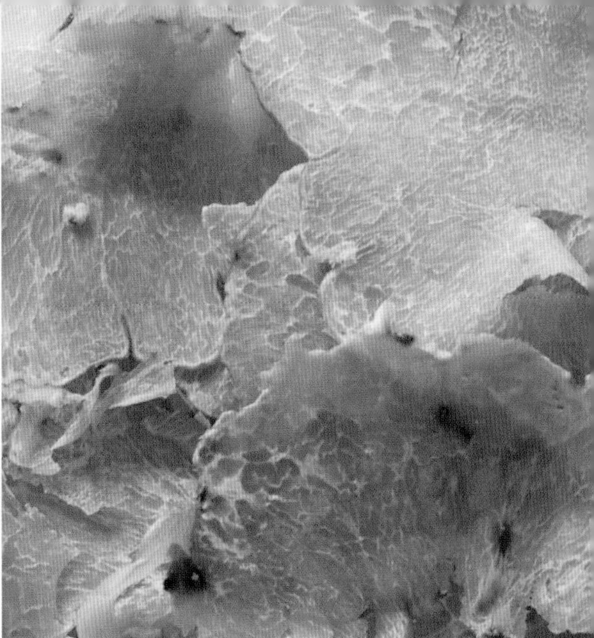

LEFT: The noble *Tuber magnatum pico* deserves a noble wine. Try the Langhe Sorì Tildìn by Angelo Gaja. BELOW: White truffles are so strongly scented that they add their flavor to eggs stored alongside. (Make sure your eggs are dry, as moisture can rot the truffle.) RIGHT: A fresh truffle, thinly shaved and gently warmed atop a bed of taglierini, releases an aroma so glorious that many call it addictive.

FILETTO DI FASSONE CON PORCINI E SALSA AL BAROLO

The *Fassone* breed of cattle holds a special place in the hearts and kitchens of northern Italian cooks. This breed, which comes from Piedmont just north of Liguria, produces meat with less than half the fat and cholesterol of most other beef, but also scant connective tissue between the muscle fibers. Translation: This beef is more tender than lean meat has a right to be. For his version of a traditional filet mignon dish, Paolo sears each tenderloin in olive oil, bathes it in sage-flavored butter, and finishes it in the oven. Try this dish once and you'll understand why it's a FARINA classic. And if you can't find U.S.-raised Piedmontese beef at your market, don't worry. Any prime- or choice-grade beef will work fine.

For recipe, see page 170.

RISERVA
1964
VINO
Barolo

LEFT: Carrots, celery, onion, garlic, herbs—think of these aromatics as the Genovese twist on mirepoix, the classic flavor base for stocks, stews, and sauces. BELOW: When meat scraps and bones hit the pan, the flavor escalates. Stir frequently to encourage the mingling that creates a rich and nuanced sauce.

ABOVE: To make the wine sauce mellow instead of bitter, Paolo stirs it over flame for just two minutes and then cooks it in the oven. RIGHT: After a journey through flame, heat, cooling, and warming, the sauce is ready to spoon over each filet. Fresh porcini mushrooms add another dimension of flavor.

LEFT: To complement this rich and complex steak dish, serve a Barolo, the aristocratic red wine from Piedmont. Try a Cascina Francia by Giacomo Conterno, with at least five years of age on it to soften the edges.

PATATE NOVELLE ARROSTO

The potato may be the backbone of *la cucina povera,* or "the poor kitchen," but to call it food for hungry peasants is to insult the potato—and the peasants. After all, hardscrabble farmers invented all those wonderful ways to enjoy these tubers, from mashed to fried to boiled to baked. Paolo especially likes the ancient art of roasting small potatoes to crisp their skins and caramelize their insides.

For recipe, see page 171.

Paolo says that the *patata quarantina bianca Genovese,* a white potato from a small town near Genoa, is the best type for roasting with herbs, butter, and olive oil. Fingerlings or red potatoes work well, too. All three of these potatoes are waxy, so they retain their moisture and shape better than starchy potatoes do.

CREMINO D'ALBA

When Paolo was fourteen, he landed his first restaurant job as the lowest helper in the kitchen, hauling sacks of flour, peeling shrimp and potatoes, and bussing dishes in the frenzy of dinner service. The chef saw promise in the young man and, after a time, taught him the ways of dessert. Paolo was particularly taken with the *cremino d'Alba,* a smooth, cool custard of cream and egg yolks thickened with gelatin and flavored with orange peel, vanilla bean, and liqueur. Today, Paolo still loves cremino. He tops it with a brittle made of caramelized sugar and hazelnuts left to harden into a translucent sheet of amber, both decorative and delicious. He serves cremino in late winter, just as the days start to lengthen. "It's primavera," he says, a forecast of spring.

For recipe, see page 172.

As an alternative to the sugar decoration at left, try candied orange slices. They're brushed with syrup and baked low and slow to a delicate crunch. See the instructions on page 41.

RECIPES

A FEW TIPS ON HOW TO COOK *LA CUCINA GENOVESE*

Genovese cooking is simple by nature, but simple isn't easy. Just ask Paolo Laboa. After an informal apprenticeship in his mother's kitchen and after thirty years behind the stove, he'll tell you that he's still learning from the ingredients, which reveal their secrets slowly. Just the same, Paolo has mastered many nuances of Genovese cuisine. Here, he tells what you'll need to succeed with the recipes that follow.

Superb Ingredients

You're only as good as your raw materials. So while a competent cook can make a decent meal out of blah ingredients, and while a fancy chef can distract diners with elaborate architecture, truly soul-satisfying food demands superior ingredients—"the freshest, the purest, the most true."

Humility

"An ingredient is like a baby in your arms," says Paolo. "You don't force it. You listen to it. You *respect*." If, for instance, your basil leaves are darker than usual, then they're stronger than usual, so use a bit less basil in your pesto to keep the flavors in balance.

The Courage of Simplicity

Many wonderful dishes have five or fewer ingredients, and take less than an hour to prepare. "But be careful," says Paolo. Simple dishes can expose any weaknesses in the ingredients or execution.

Flexibility

"Don't be a slave to any recipe—not even mine," says Paolo. A recipe is like sheet music. Once you learn to play the melody, you can improvise, making small adjustments to suit changing ingredients or changing weather. And whatever you do, don't take a recipe with you to the market. Instead, wander around. What looks freshest? What smells best? Buy it. *Then* go home and find a recipe, or make up your own. With steady practice, you'll be surprised at how quickly you learn and how delicious your cooking can be.

Love

"Once, when I was a boy, I asked, 'Mama, why do you sing when you cook?' She said, 'If you're happy when you cook, your food is happy.'"

Nota Bene:

- "Water is the foundation. It must be clean and neutral in flavor." Does this mean you might have to cook even your pasta in filtered water? *"Sì!"* By the way, boil your pasta in water that is "as salty as the sea." Pasta cooked this way tastes good—not salty.
- Most of the recipes call for coarse sea salt. Try a few brands until you find your favorite.
- Fresh yeast tastes best and works fastest, but dry active yeast is more readily available, and it works fine.
- Extra-virgin olive oil loses its subtle and complex flavors when subjected to high heat, so use it only in recipes where it will be heated gently or not heated at all. For high heat, plain olive oil is fine.
- Just before serving nearly any savory dish, sprinkle it with extra-virgin olive oil. It makes a fragrant and flavorful addition.

SPRING | ANTIPASTO

FOCACCINA GENOVESE CON PROSCIUTTO DI PARMA E BURRATA

Focaccia with Prosciutto and Burrata | *Serves 4*

Featured on p. 16

In this "little focaccia" bread, a signature dish at FARINA, fresh sage matters. "It cuts the fat and refreshes the palate," says Paolo.

- 1 T active dry yeast
- 1/2 c warm water
- 2 c all-purpose flour
- 1 T chopped fresh sage
- 1/2 t coarse sea salt
- 1 c olive oil
- 1/2 lb sliced prosciutto di Parma or other prosciutto (3 or 4 slices for each person)
- 8 oz burrata cheese

In a small bowl, dissolve yeast in water. Let sit 5 to 10 minutes until foamy. In another bowl, combine flour, sage, salt. Add the yeast mixture to the flour mixture and knead, by hand, for 3 to 5 minutes, until dough is free of lumps. Place the dough in a lightly oiled bowl, cover and put aside in a warm place to rise for about 1 hour. The dough should double in size.

Turn the dough onto a floured work surface and divide in half. Roll each half into a ball, cover, and let rest for 10 minutes. Then, taking one ball at a time, stretch and flatten the dough with your palms, using your fingers to push the dough outward to form a rough circle about 1/2 inch thick and 8 to 9 inches across.

Heat 1 cup of olive oil in a 12-inch pan over medium-high heat. When the oil is hot but not so hot that it burns, fry each dough circle for 2 minutes on each side, then blot on paper towels and sprinkle with coarse sea salt to taste. To serve, place each focaccina on a plate—in this case, you'll make two plates to serve four people. Top each focaccina with half of the prosciutto slices and half of the burrata. Serve immediately.

SPRING | PANE

PANE AL ROSMARINO

Rosemary Bread | *Makes 2 loaves*

Featured on p. 22

Look for large, plump rosemary needles. If you can find only thin needles that taste faintly of lemon, reduce their quantity to 2 tablespoons so as not to overpower the bread. Tip: If you'd like to see rosemary on the surface of your bread, sprinkle (or press) roughly chopped rosemary on the top just before the second rise.

- 1 t active dry yeast
- 3/4 c warm water
- 3 1/4 c starter (p. 173)
- 3 c unbleached bread flour
- 1 3/4 t coarse sea salt
- 3 T chopped fresh rosemary

In a small bowl, dissolve yeast in water. Let sit 5 to 10 minutes until foamy. In the bowl of your stand mixer, combine the starter, flour, and yeast mixture. Using the dough hook, mix on low for 5 minutes and then check the consistency; it should be tacky but not sticky. If necessary, add a bit more water or flour. (Paolo likes our dough to be on the wet side because it makes the bread more chewy.) Then add the salt and rosemary and mix on medium speed for 3 minutes. Place the dough in a lightly oiled bowl, cover, and put aside in a warm place to rise for about 1 hour. The dough should double in size.

Turn the dough onto a floured work surface and divide in half. Shape into rounds, cover, and let rest for 15 minutes. Then shape into narrow oblong loaves.

Place the loaves on a baking sheet, cover, and allow to rise for 45 minutes to 1 hour. Press the dough gently. If your fingerprint remains, it's ready. If your fingerprint pops back quickly, wait a few more minutes.

Heat oven to 425°F. With a knife, make a cut about 1/2 inch deep lengthwise down the center of each loaf. (This enables the loaves to expand without cracking.) Place loaves in the oven and spritz with water to create the steam that makes a crunchy, shiny crust. Reduce heat to 400°F and bake for 25 minutes. Check sides and bottom; if not hard and dark tan, leave in oven for another 10 minutes, then check again. Transfer loaves to a rack to cool for 30 minutes before slicing.

CAPPELLACCI DI MELANZANE E ZUCCHINI AL BURRO E TIMO

Cappellacci Filled with Eggplant and Zucchini | *Serves 4*

Featured on p. 26

Cappellacci is a filled pasta similar to ravioli. In Paolo's twist on his mother's recipe, the Brie is the key: It's slightly bitter at the start, like the eggplant, and it's sweet at the finish, like the zucchini. Tip: "When you make the filling, let the oil run off," says Paolo. "When you get too much fat in the filling, it's too loose, like mayonnaise."

Filling

1 small eggplant, about 1/2 lb

2 small zucchini, about 1/2 lb

2 T chopped onion

1 small clove garlic, minced

1/2 t coarse sea salt

1 T chopped fresh marjoram

3 oz Brie (rind removed), sliced

2 T finely grated Parmigiano-Reggiano cheese

Basic Pasta Dough (p. 173)

4 T (1/2 stick) unsalted butter

1/2 t chopped fresh thyme

1-1/2 T and pinch coarse sea salt, divided

Parmigiano-Reggiano cheese, coarsely grated, for serving

To make the filling: Peel the eggplant. Cut both eggplant and zucchini into 1/4-inch slices. In a large pan over medium-high heat, pour just enough olive oil to cover the surface, and then add the eggplant, zucchini, onion, garlic, salt, and marjoram. Cook until soft, stirring occasionally. Add the Brie and stir to melt. Transfer mixture to a food processor and pulse until smooth. Then stir in the Parmigiano-Reggiano. If you see any oil collecting on the surface, pour it off and discard. Set filling aside to cool.

To form the cappellacci: Feed the pasta dough 3 or 4 times through the widest setting of a pasta machine. Then move the roller to the next narrower notch and pass the dough through twice. Continue 2 passes on each successive notch until you can almost see your hand through the pasta sheet. Cut the sheet in half crosswise. Place one of the halves on a floured surface. Place a heaping teaspoon of cooled filling at regular intervals —about 2 inches apart—on the sheet (see photo, p. 28). Place the other pasta sheet on top and gently press down on the pasta surrounding each dollop of filling. Cut out the resulting pasta pillows with a round cookie cutter 3 to 4 inches across. Press the edges gently to secure the filling.

Fill a large pot with water and place it over high heat to boil. As the water warms, stir in 1-1/2 tablespoons coarse sea salt. Gently drop the cappellacci into the boiling water and cook for 2 to 3 minutes until it's *al dente*. Drain. While the pasta cooks, heat butter in a skillet until it is light brown. As butter is browning, add the thyme and pinch of coarse sea salt. To serve, divide the pasta among 4 plates, spoon on the butter sauce, and sprinkle with Parmigiano-Reggiano. Serve immediately.

TAGLIATA DI TONNO CON ASPARAGI, SPUMA DI BURRATA, E RIDUZIONE D'AGLIANICO

Yellowfin Tuna with Asparagus, Burrata Mousse, and Aglianico Reduction | *Serves 4*

Featured on p. 32

Dense and substantial, yellowfin tuna is the ocean's answer to red meat. In this dish, Paolo prepares the tuna with juniper berries and serves it with a mousse, or spuma, *of burrata cheese whipped with olive oil. The juniper intensifies the tuna while the cheese complements its sweetness. Tip from Paolo: "If you want to please the tuna, don't overcook it."*

Marinade

1 c extra-virgin olive oil

1 T fresh oregano (or 1 t dried)

1 T chopped fresh basil

1 t juniper berries

pinch red chili flakes

1/2 t coarse sea salt

Aglianico Reduction

1-1/2 cups Aglianico (or another light, acidic, fruity red wine)

2 t sugar

Burrata Mousse

8 oz burrata cheese (or fresh buffalo mozzarella)

extra-virgin olive oil

pinch coarse sea salt

12 stalks asparagus

4 fresh yellowfin tuna steaks, 5 to 6 oz each

To make the marinade: Pour the olive oil into a shallow dish. In a mortar, mash together the herbs, juniper berries, chili flakes, and salt. Add to olive oil, stirring to combine. Add the tuna steaks, turning to coat them in the marinade. Refrigerate, covered, 1 to 2 hours.

To make the Aglianico reduction: In a small saucepan over medium heat, combine wine, sugar, and 2 tablespoons of water. When the mixture reaches a simmer, turn heat to low and cook, stirring often, until syrupy, about 9 minutes. Remove from heat; it will thicken further as it cools. (If made in advance, the reduction will keep in the refrigerator, covered, for at least 3 weeks. If you refrigerate it, let it sit out for at least an hour to take the chill off before using.)

To make the burrata mousse: Whisk by hand or blend in a food processor the burrata cheese and just enough extra-virgin olive oil to achieve a thick (not runny) purée. Add a pinch of coarse sea salt.

To make the asparagus: Clean the stalks and peel them if they're thick or tough. Blanch them in salted boiling water for 15 seconds. Drain and place in a shallow dish. Cover and cool in the refrigerator. Just before serving, sauté the stalks in a hot pan with a bit of olive oil.

To cook the tuna: Heat oven to 450°F. Place a large, ovenproof fry pan over medium heat on the stove. Add enough olive oil to coat the pan and wait for it to shimmer. Remove tuna steaks from marinade and pat dry. Cook on one side for 2 minutes, turn tuna gently, and place the pan in the oven for an additional 2 minutes. Remove tuna steaks from the pan, let them rest for 1 minute, and then slice them across the grain.

To serve, nestle tuna, asparagus, and burrata mousse near the center of each plate. Drizzle Aglianico reduction and extra-virgin olive oil along the edge. Serve immediately.

SPRING | CONTORNO

CIME DI PISELLI SALTATI ALL'OLIO D'OLIVA

Pea Tendrils with Olive Oil | *Serves 4*

Featured on p. 38

Pea tendrils, or shoots, are the leaves, strings, and stems from young pea plants—the excess foliage that farmers trim off. Look for them at farmers' markets or at Asian groceries. A simple preparation is the best way to let the tendrils express their subtly sweet flavor.

1 bunch pea tendrils, about 1/2 lb
2 T olive oil
pinch red chili flakes
pinch coarse sea salt

Rinse and drain the tendrils. Heat a fry pan over medium heat and then add the oil and chili flakes. Stir in the tendrils and salt. Cook, stirring frequently, 3 to 5 minutes until tendrils are wilted and soft. Serve immediately.

SPRING | DOLCE

LATTE DOLCE FRITTO

Sweet Milk Fritters | *Serves 4*

Featured on p. 40

Genoa, being near France, is mad for pastry, and "every nonna knows how to make sweet milk fritters," says Paolo. The important thing in this dessert is to whisk without stopping. "Be patient. Stay and stir." Tip: If you want to make these fritters one or two days ahead, stop just after breading them and then refrigerate, covered. Fry them just before you serve.

Batter

2 c whole milk
1 cinnamon stick (or 1/2 t cinnamon)
zest from 1/2 orange
1 vanilla bean, split lengthwise (or 1 t vanilla extract)
pinch coarse sea salt
1/4 c all-purpose flour
1/4 c sugar
2 large eggs, beaten

Breading

1/4 c all-purpose flour
1 large egg, beaten
1/2 c fine dry bread crumbs
1/4 c grapeseed oil (or other neutral, high-heat oil such as canola)
1/2 c sugar
orange segments for garnish

Butter a 8 x 4-inch loaf pan. In a 1-1/2-quart saucepan (preferably with a 6-inch diameter), combine milk, cinnamon, orange zest, vanilla, and salt. Bring to a gentle simmer over medium heat. In a mixing bowl, combine 1/4 cup each flour and sugar. Strain the milk into the flour-and-sugar mixture and whisk to combine. Return to the saucepan and place back on the stove over medium-high heat. Whisk continuously for 12 minutes. The mixture will thicken and bubble. Lower the heat if it starts to stick. Take the pan off the heat, add the beaten eggs, and whisk vigorously for 30 seconds. Then place back on the heat and whisk steadily for another 7 minutes until batter is thick and free of lumps. Pour batter into the greased pan and smooth the top with a spatula or spoon. Refrigerate for about 2 hours or until batter feels firm on top and the dish feels cold.

To bread and fry the fritters: Flip batter out onto a cutting board and cut into 8 squares. Set out 3 bowls and fill the first with the flour, the second with the beaten egg, and the third with the bread crumbs. Put the sugar on a plate and set aside. Coat each square with flour, then egg, then bread crumbs. Heat the oil in a fry pan over medium-high heat and fry the squares, 4 at a time, just enough to toast the bread crumbs, about 1 minute per side. Place the hot squares on the plate of sugar and toss gently. To serve, place 2 squares on each plate. Garnish with orange segments and, if you wish, with candied orange slices (see p. 41).

Note: At FARINA, Paolo often serves the fritters with a simple orange sauce. To make it combine 1 cup fresh-squeezed orange juice and 1/4 cup sugar in a small saucepan. Boil, stirring, until the sauce is thickened and "like velvet." Refrigerate the sauce and serve when cool.

CAPESANTE ROSTICCIATE CON COLINO DI POMODORI E OLIO AL BASILICO

Seared Scallops with Tomato Essence and Basil Oil | *Serves 4*

Featured on p. 48

For many generations, everyone in Genoa baked their scallops with cheese in a gratinée. But then someone decided to preserve the fresh-from-the sea flavor of scallops with a quick sear in a hot pan. While we still like the gratinée, we prefer this dish. The tomato essence and basil oil taste like liquid summertime. Tip: Instead of blanching the basil—which can leach its flavor—Paolo sweats it in oil and then dry-cools the mixture over ice.

Tomato Essence

1 or 2 vine-ripe tomatoes, about 1/2 lb

1 T olive oil

1-1/2 t chopped fresh thyme

1/8 t coarse sea salt

cheesecloth

Basil Oil

1/4 c grapeseed oil (or other neutral oil such as canola)

1/4 c olive oil

1/4 c basil leaves (preferably *Ocimum basilicum 'Genovese'*), loosely packed, rinsed, and dried

1/8 t coarse sea salt

Scallops

12 fresh day-boat sea scallops

2 T olive oil

To make the tomato essence: Heat oven to 450°F. Slice tomatoes in half and place cut side up on a cookie sheet. Drizzle olive oil over tomatoes and sprinkle with thyme and salt. Roast tomatoes about 30 to 40 minutes until very soft. Wrap tomatoes in cheesecloth, tie with twine, and hang them over a bowl for 1 hour until all the tomato essence drains into the bowl. (You can suspend the tomatoes from a wooden spoon placed across the bowl's rim.)

To make the basil oil: Heat the grapeseed oil and olive oil over medium heat. Add the basil leaves and cook for 5 minutes, stirring occasionally. Pour the basil and oil mixture into a metal bowl that is nestled in a bed of ice. When cool, purée with the salt in a blender until smooth. Strain through a coffee filter or fine-mesh sieve to render a clear oil.

Clean the scallops by peeling off and discarding the muscle on the side. Rinse with cold water to remove any sand, then pat dry. (You need dry scallops because you want to sear them, not steam them.) Place a pan on high heat, wait a few moments, and then add the olive oil. When the oil shimmers, carefully place the scallops in the pan, leaving space between them so that vapor can escape. Don't move the scallops. Let them sear for about 2 minutes until medium-brown. Then turn them gently and sear the other side for 2 or 3 minutes until medium-rare and just opaque.

To serve, place a few spoonfuls of tomato essence on a plate, then top with the seared scallops straight from the pan. Drizzle scallops with basil oil. Serve immediately.

PANE CON OLIVE TAGGIASCHE

Olive Bread | *Makes 2 loaves*

Featured on p. 54

Developed long ago by Benedictine monks near the town of Taggia, the Taggiasca olive is a pride of Liguria. It's small in size and gently sweet, and in addition to making an olive oil famous for its delicate and complex flavor, it's good for eating—and for baking into this olive bread. If you can't find Taggiasche olives, Niçoise will also work.

1 t active dry yeast

3/4 c warm water

3 1/4 c starter (p. 173)

3 c unbleached bread flour

1 3/4 t coarse sea salt

1/2 c Taggiasche olives, pits removed

In a small bowl, dissolve yeast in water. Let sit 5 to 10 minutes until foamy. In the bowl of your stand mixer, combine the starter, flour, and yeast mixture. Using the dough hook, mix on low for 5 minutes and then check the consistency; it should be tacky but not sticky. If necessary, add a bit more water or flour. (Paolo likes our dough to be on the wet side because it makes the bread more chewy.) Then add the salt and olives and mix on medium speed for 3 minutes. Place the dough in a lightly oiled bowl, cover, and put aside in a warm place to rise for about 1 hour. The dough should double in size.

Turn the dough onto a floured work surface and divide in half. Shape into rounds, cover, and let rest for 15 minutes. Then shape into narrow oblong loaves.

Place the loaves on a baking sheet, cover, and allow to rise for 45 minutes to 1 hour. Press the dough gently. If your fingerprint remains, the dough is ready for baking. If your fingerprint pops back quickly, wait a few more minutes.

Heat oven to 425°F. With a knife, make 3 diagonal cuts about 1/2 inch deep along the length of each loaf. (This enables the loaves to expand without cracking.) Place loaves in the oven and spritz with water to create the steam that makes a crunchy, shiny crust. Reduce heat to 400°F and bake for 25 minutes. Check sides and bottom; if not hard and dark tan, leave in oven for another 10 minutes, then check again. Transfer loaves to a rack to cool for 30 minutes before slicing.

MANDILLI DI SETA AL PESTO GENOVESE

Silk Handkerchief Pasta with Genovese Basil Pesto | *Serves 4*

Featured on p. 60

Once you try Paolo's silk handkerchief pasta with basil pesto, you'll see why it won the Pesto World Championship in Genoa. The texture is smooth and the flavors are balanced, so instead of a sharp and chunky sauce, you get something light and clean. The secret is the Genovese basil, soaked in cold water to soften the flavor. Note: Below, we give directions for making the pesto in a blender, but you can also make it in a large mortar.

Basil Pesto Genovese

4 c basil leaves (preferably *Ocimum basilicum 'Genovese'*), loosely packed

1/3 c pine nuts

1/2 c extra-virgin olive oil

1/2 t chopped fresh garlic

1 t coarse sea salt

1/3 c finely grated Parmigiano-Reggiano cheese

1/3 c finely grated aged pecorino cheese

Basic Pasta Dough (p. 173)

1-1/2 T coarse sea salt

coarsely grated Parmigiano-Reggiano cheese, for serving

4 basil leaves, for garnish

To make the pesto: Wash the basil in cold water. Gently pinch leaves from stems. Soak the leaves in a bowl of cold water for 1 hour.

Put the pine nuts, olive oil, and garlic in a blender. Pulse to make a coarse paste. Add basil leaves 1 cup at a time, shaking off some but not all of the water (a little water helps the ingredients to emulsify). Pulse a few times after each addition. When all of the basil has been puréed, add the salt and blend on high until the pesto is smooth. Add the cheeses and pulse to blend. (Take care not to overblend the pesto at this stage or it will heat up and separate like a broken sauce.) Pour the pesto into a broad, medium-sized mixing bowl. If more than 20 minutes before serving, cover pesto with a thin film of mild olive oil to slow oxidation.

To make the mandilli: Feed the pasta dough 3 or 4 times through the widest setting of a pasta machine. Then move the roller to the next narrower notch and pass the dough through twice. Continue 2 passes on each successive notch until you can almost see your hand through the pasta sheet. Cut the pasta sheets into handkerchiefs about 6 inches square.

Fill a large pot with water and place it over high heat to boil. As the water warms, stir in the salt. Drop the pasta gently into the boiling water and cook until *al dente*, testing after 2 minutes. As the pasta cooks, scoop up a tablespoon of the hot pasta water and stir it into the bowl of pesto to melt the cheese and meld the ingredients. (Never heat pesto over a flame. High heat kills the flavor.) Add the cooked, drained pasta to the bowl of pesto and stir each handkerchief gently to coat. Place pasta and any remaining pesto on plates. Top each serving with a few sprinkles of Parmigiano-Reggiano and a basil leaf. Serve immediately.

DENTICE IN BRODETTO CON CARCIOFI

Whole Thai Snapper with Artichokes in a Broth | *Serves 4*

Featured on p. 70

Dentice, or Thai snapper, is a lot like branzino: dense and firm, so it's a good dish when you don't want something heavy but do want some substance on your plate. Tip: Buy the freshest fish you can find. Look for clear eyes, firm flesh, and sparkly iridescence. By the way, Paolo's mother cooked fish in terracotta and copper, and she dedicated specific pans to fish and fish broth. So does Paolo. The pans transmit an essence that you can't buy.

1 T lemon juice

1 T flour

4 medium-large artichokes

8 T olive oil, divided

1-1/2 cloves garlic, divided

3 bay leaves, divided

1 c plus 2 T white wine

whole fresh Thai snapper or branzino, about 3 lb

1/4 medium onion, roughly chopped

1/4 medium carrot, roughly chopped

1/2 medium stalk celery, roughly chopped

1/2 c flat-leaf parsley, stemmed

3 sprigs thyme

4 basil leaves

2 plum tomatoes, fresh or canned, crushed

To prepare the artichokes: Fill a medium-large bowl with about 4 inches of water. Stir in the lemon juice and flour. Set aside. Peel away the outer leaves of the artichokes until you reach the pale, smaller, softer leaves. Slice off the top 1/3 or so to remove any sharp points on the tips of the leaves, and trim all but about 1/2 inch of stem. Then, using a serrated bread knife, slice each artichoke in half lengthwise and remove both the choke and the purple-tipped leaves that surround it. It can help to use a spoon or a melon baller to remove every trace of tough fiber. Once you've cleaned each artichoke, place it in the bowl of water with lemon and flour to preserve the color.

Heat a large pot over medium heat and add 2 tablespoons olive oil, 1/2 smashed garlic clove, and 2 bay leaves. Then add the artichokes, cut sides up, plus enough water to just cover. Add 2 tablespoons wine and sprinkle with coarse sea salt to taste. Simmer, covered, for 10 to 12 minutes until stems are tender when poked with a knife. Remove artichokes from pot and let cool.

To prepare the dentice and the brodetto: Heat oven to 375°F. Rinse the fish. Make a lengthwise cut about 1/2 inch deep along the thickest part of the fish on each side. In a roasting pan or large ovenproof skillet, combine 1 smashed garlic clove, 1 bay leaf, onion, carrot, celery, parsley, thyme, basil, tomatoes, 4 tablespoons olive oil, 1 cup wine, and 1 cup water. Add the fish. Cook uncovered in the oven for about 20 minutes, and then check fish for doneness along the cut. The fish should be white and opaque. If it's still translucent, pop the fish back into the oven for about 3 minutes. When done, transfer fish to a warmed serving platter. Strain the remaining brodetto, or "little broth," into a small pot. Add coarse sea salt if needed. Keep warm.

While the fish is in the oven, crisp the artichokes: Place a sauté pan over high heat, then add the remaining 2 tablespoons of olive oil. When hot, add the artichoke halves, cut sides down. Sauté 3 or 4 minutes, turning the artichokes occasionally to crisp them evenly.

To serve, pour a few tablespoons of brodetto over the fish on the platter. Place the artichokes alongside. Serve with bread to sop up the brodetto.

MELANZANE ALLA PARMIGIANA

Eggplant Parmigiana | *Serves 4*

Featured on p. 76

If it's been a while since you've had eggplant parmesan, try this one. It may remind you why this dish became a classic. Tip: Choose an eggplant that's light for its size. An eggplant that's heavy with seeds is more apt to be bitter. Note that you'll need to salt the eggplant and let it drain overnight before proceeding with this dish, so plan accordingly.

Tomato Sauce

28-oz can San Marzano tomatoes (or other whole peeled plum tomatoes)

1 clove garlic, smashed

a few basil leaves (preferably *Ocimum basilicum 'Genovese'*)

1 medium eggplant, about 2/3 lb

all-purpose flour, for dredging

1/2 c grapeseed oil (or other neutral, high-heat oil such as canola)

1 c coarsely grated Parmigiano-Reggiano cheese

4-oz ball fresh mozzarella, cut in half and sliced very thin

20 basil leaves (preferably *Ocimum basilicum 'Genovese'*), plus more for garnish

a few pinches dried oregano

sprinkles of coarse sea salt

Wash and dry the eggplant. Cut off stem end and slice eggplant crosswise into 1/4-inch rounds. Sprinkle each slice lightly with coarse sea salt. Place the slices in a colander and let them rest overnight in the refrigerator, where they will release some of their liquid and much of their bitterness.

To make the tomato sauce: Whirl tomatoes in a blender until smooth. Place a fry pan over medium-high heat and coat the bottom with olive oil. When the oil shimmers, add the smashed garlic clove and stir for about 1 minute to flavor the oil. Discard garlic. Add basil leaves and stir gently for about 10 seconds. Then stir in the puréed tomatoes. When the sauce starts to bubble, turn down heat and simmer for 15 to 20 minutes. Season with coarse sea salt to taste. Set aside.

To prepare the eggplant: Use a towel to brush off any excess salt. Then dredge each slice in flour to coat lightly. Place a fry pan over high heat and add the 1/2 cup oil. When the oil shimmers, add the eggplant slices; they should sizzle. Fry a few slices at a time until golden brown, adding oil if necessary. Do not crowd the pan. Place the fried slices on paper towels to drain.

Heat oven to 375°F. In a baking dish about 8 x 5 x 2 inches, layer the following: 1/4 cup of tomato sauce, a generous sprinkling of Parmigiano-Reggiano, 1 layer of mozzarella slices, 4 or 5 basil leaves, a pinch of oregano, a sprinkle of coarse sea salt, and 1 layer of eggplant slices. Continue to layer in this sequence. Finish with a topping of mozzarella, basil leaves, and a sprinkle of olive oil. Bake for 15 to 20 minutes until bubbling hot. Remove from oven and allow to rest for at least 5 minutes before serving, or serve at room temperature. Garnish each serving with a basil leaf.

CESTINO DI PASTA MATTA CON FRAGOLE

Cookie Baskets with Mascarpone Cream and Strawberries | *Serves 4*

Featured on p. 78

Paolo says that the season for chocolate desserts is October until Easter. Come spring, you want something lighter, such as a tuile cestino, *or basket. Neutral in flavor and crunchy in texture, it makes an excellent vehicle for mascarpone cream with strawberries. Tip: You can prepare the baskets in advance and keep them in a cookie jar for up to ten hours before serving. And when you make the baskets, don't worry if they're not perfect. "The first is always the worst," says Paolo, "and it will still taste good."*

Tuiles

- 4 T (1/2 stick) unsalted butter
- 1/2 c minus 1 T confectioners' sugar
- 1/2 c minus 1 T all-purpose flour
- 1/4 c egg whites (from 2 or 3 eggs, depending on size)

Cream Filling

- 3 large egg yolks
- 1/4 c sugar
- 2 T Grand Marnier
- 6 oz mascarpone cheese, at room temperature
- 1/4 c egg whites (from 2 or 3 eggs, depending on size)
- 1 pint strawberries, sliced

confectioners' sugar, for garnish

To make the tuiles: Melt the butter and then let it cool to room temperature. Then whisk the butter with the sugar, flour, and egg whites until smooth. Rest batter in the refrigerator, covered, for 20 minutes.

Heat oven to 400°F. Line a cookie sheet with a silicone baking mat or parchment paper. Have ready 2 teacups or small bowls placed upside down and next to each other on your work surface. Using a soup spoon or table-spoon, scoop one spoonful of the cooled batter onto the center of the cookie sheet and then, with a spatula, smooth the batter into a thin disk about 5 inches across. Bake for 2 or 3 minutes until it's tan on the edges. Remove the cookie sheet from the oven, carefully remove the hot disk, and drape it over one inverted teacup. Gently place the second inverted teacup on top of the disk. After about 30 seconds, the disk will be cool. Carefully remove the top teacup and you'll have a "cookie basket." Repeat this cookie-making procedure until you have 4 baskets.

To make the cream filling: In a double boiler or a metal bowl placed just above simmering water, gently whisk together the egg yolks, sugar, and Grand Marnier. Whisk continu-ously just until the sugar dissolves. Remove the mixture from the heat and whisk until it doubles in volume and lightens in color. Then gently fold in the mascarpone. In a separate bowl, whisk egg whites to stiff peaks and then fold into the mascarpone mixture. Cool in the refrigerator for at least 10 minutes.

To assemble: Spoon the cream filling into the baskets. Top each basket with strawberry slices and sprinkle with confectioners' sugar. Serve immediately.

Note: To make the optional sugar spiral decorations, combine 1/2 cup sugar and 1/4 cup water in a small saucepan. Place the pan over high heat and swirl it gently. In about a minute, the mixture will bubble and the sugar will start to caramelize. When the sugar looks like dark amber maple syrup, add a few drops of lemon juice, stir, and take the pan off the heat. (The lemon helps keep the sugar malleable, but you'll still only have about 2 minutes to shape it.) Take a spoonful of hot syrup and drizzle a thin strand onto a knife-honing steel, slowly spinning the steel to create a corkscrew spiral of sugar (see photo, p. 80). Taking care not to burn yourself, nudge the spiral with your fingers to create a pleasing shape. Wait until spiral cools and then gently slide it off the steel. Repeat. If the sugar gets too hard to shape, reheat it.

CALAMARI AL PIGATO CON PATATA SCHIACCIATA ALLO ZAFFERANO

Calamari with Saffron Mashed Potatoes | *Serves 4*

Featured on p. 86

When Paolo was eight years old, he tried his first calamari—raw with a sprinkle of salt, a squeeze of lemon, and a few drops of extra-virgin olive oil. In this dish, he preserves the fresh flavor of the calamari while adding the exotic comfort of puréed potatoes flavored with saffron. Tip: Get good saffron from the La Mancha region of Spain, and then go easy on it. A pinch will do.

Saffron Mashed Potatoes

2 to 3 medium-sized russet potatoes (or other starchy potatoes), about 1-1/4 lb

3/4 c whole milk

3/4 t coarse sea salt

pinch saffron

Calamari

2 T olive oil

1 clove garlic, finely chopped

pinch red chili flakes

2 pinches coarse sea salt

1 lb calamari (bodies and tentacles), cleaned

1/2 c Pigato (or other light white wine)

To make the mashed potatoes: Peel the potatoes and cut in half. Boil them until fully cooked, then smash with a masher or put through a ricer. Heat milk with the salt and saffron over medium heat, stirring, until just shy of boiling. Add the milk to the potatoes and mix well with a wooden spoon. Keep warm.

To cook the calamari: Heat a pan on high heat and add the olive oil. Stir in the garlic, chili flakes, and salt. Add the calamari carefully, so as not to splash hot oil. Cook for 60 to 90 seconds, stirring gently, and then add the wine. Cook for just 1 more minute until the calamari are pale brown. To serve, spoon the potatoes onto serving plates and top with the calamari and pan juices. Serve immediately.

PANE DI PATATE

Potato Bread | *Makes 2 rounds*

Featured on p. 92

Being abundant and inexpensive, potatoes are a staple of la cucina contadina, *or the country kitchen. Here, they add their fluffy starch and subtle flavor to bread.*

- 1 t active dry yeast
- 3/4 c warm water
- 3 1/4 c starter (p. 173)
- 3 c unbleached bread flour
- 1 3/4 t coarse sea salt
- 2 medium-sized russet potatoes (or other starchy potatoes), about 1 lb, peeled, boiled, and mashed
- 2 T chopped fresh rosemary

In a small bowl, dissolve yeast in water. Let sit 5 to 10 minutes until foamy. In the bowl of your stand mixer, combine the starter, flour, and yeast mixture. Using the dough hook, mix on low for 5 minutes and then check the consistency; it should be tacky but not sticky. If necessary, add a bit more water or flour. (Paolo likes our dough to be on the wet side because it makes the bread more chewy.) Then add the salt, potatoes, and rosemary; mix on medium speed for 3 minutes. Place the dough in a lightly oiled bowl, cover, and put aside in a warm place to rise for about 1 hour. The dough should double in size.

Turn the dough onto a floured work surface and divide in half. Shape into rounds, cover, and let dough rest for 15 minutes. Then transfer the rounds to two 9-inch round cake pans, cover, and allow to rise for 45 minutes to 1 hour. Press the dough gently. If your fingerprint remains, the dough is ready. If your fingerprint pops back quickly, wait a few more minutes.

Heat oven to 425°F. Place pans in the oven and spritz the rounds with water to create the steam that makes a crunchy, shiny crust. Reduce heat to 400°F and bake for 25 to 35 minutes. The rounds are done when they pull away from the sides of the pans and the tops are evenly browned and feel firm when tapped. Transfer the pans to cool on a rack for 10 minutes. Then turn the rounds out of their pans to cool on a rack for 30 more minutes before slicing.

Note: To make bread that contains discernible potato chunks in addition to mashed potatoes in the dough, do as Paolo often does. He slices a few small, waxy potatoes 1/4 inch thick and parboils them for 3 or 4 minutes to remove some starch. Then, after 35 minutes of the second rise, he gently slices off the top of each doughy loaf and arranges the potato slices in a single layer, along with a few sage leaves. He then puts the "lid" of dough back on the loaf and allows it to rise for about 15 more minutes before baking.

PAPPARDELLE AL ROSMARINO CON FUNGHI PORCINI

Rosemary Papparadelle with Porcini Mushrooms | *Serves 4*

Featured on p. 96

From late summer through October, a young Paolo and his uncle and brother roamed the hills outside Genoa in search of the porcini, "the best mushroom you can eat, and impossible to farm." The dirt near porcini mushrooms smells faintly like rosemary, says Paolo, and they often grow near each other. Using the principle of "what grows together, goes together," Paolo pairs rosemary and porcini in this dish. Tip: Look for large, plump rosemary needles and chop them small. If you can find only thin needles that taste faintly of lemons or lavender, reduce their quantity to 1 teaspoon so as not to overpower the dish.

Pappardelle

2 c Caputo brand "00" flour (or all-purpose flour)

2 large eggs, at room temperature

3 large egg yolks, at room temperature

1-1/2 t chopped fresh rosemary

1-1/2 T coarse sea salt

Sautéed Porcini Mushrooms

2 T olive oil

1/2 lb medium-sized porcini mushrooms, sliced thinly

1 t finely chopped garlic

1 T chopped flat-leaf parsley

To make the pappardelle: Mound the flour on a cutting board or counter and make a deep well in the center. Pour the eggs, yolks, and rosemary into the well and beat lightly with a fork for 20 seconds. Then gradually push dry flour into the well, stirring in a circular motion with your fingers, until you have a single ball of dough. Press your thumb into the ball. If the dough sticks to your thumb, add a bit more flour. When your thumb comes away clean, the dough is ready to knead. Knead dough for 7 to 9 minutes until smooth.

Divide the dough in half and then feed each piece into a pasta machine, starting on the widest setting. Pass each piece through 4 times, then move the roller to the next narrower notch and pass the dough through twice. Continue 2 passes on each successive notch until the dough is slightly thinner than a lasagna noodle. Let the pasta sheets hang for 5 minutes to dry, or lay them out flat for 5 minutes on each side.

While the pasta dries, fill a large pot with water and place it over high heat to boil. As the water warms, stir in the salt.

Dust each pasta sheet with flour and then cut into broad ribbons about 2 inches wide and 6 inches long. Gently drop the ribbons into the boiling, salted water and cook until *al dente*, testing after 2 minutes. Drain pasta and set aside, reserving about 1/2 cup of the cooking water.

To cook the mushrooms: Place a fry pan or sauté pan over medium-high heat. The pan should be large enough to hold the mushrooms plus the pasta without crowding. Add the oil and wait for it to shimmer. Add mushrooms and sauté lightly for 3 to 4 minutes; don't brown them or their subtle flavor will suffer. Add garlic and parsley, plus coarse sea salt to taste. Cook for 1 more minute.

Add the pasta to your pan of mushrooms and toss over medium heat to mix them. If the mixture seems dry, add a spoonful of hot pasta water. The water and oil will emulsify to make a bit of light sauce. Serve immediately.

TENERO D'AGNELLO LARDELLATO AL TARTUFO NERO

Lamb Filled with Black Truffles | *Serves 4*

Featured on p. 102

The black truffles in this dish temper the lamb's gaminess and enhance its flavor at the same time. "The filling is an infusion," says Paolo. "It flavors the meat from the inside out." Serve with sauce on top and with the roasted potatoes on page 171.

7 T olive oil, divided

1/2 onion and 1/2 carrot, roughly chopped

1 stalk celery, roughly chopped

2 cloves garlic, whole

4 bay leaves

5 cloves

20 juniper berries

1 long sprig rosemary (about 6 inches)

5 sprigs flat-leaf parsley

2 lb rack of lamb, boned and cut into 4 loins (save the bones and trimmings)

2 c dry white wine

1 t tomato paste

6 whole peeled plum tomatoes (canned)

.8–.9 oz (25 grams) fresh black truffles

1-1/2 t chopped fresh marjoram

7 oz pancetta

2 1/2 T extra-virgin olive oil

all-purpose flour, for dusting

1 T unsalted butter

2 sage leaves

To make the sauce: Place a medium lidded saucepan (about 10 inches round, or oval equivalent) over medium heat. Heat 2 tablespoons olive oil and then stir in the onion, carrot, celery, and garlic. Add the bay leaves, cloves, juniper berries, rosemary sprig, and parsley, followed by the lamb bones and trimmings. Season with coarse sea salt. Cook for 10 minutes, stirring frequently. Combine wine and tomato paste, add to pan, lower heat, and simmer for 5 minutes. Stir in the plum tomatoes and simmer for another 5 minutes. Add 1 cup water and cover pan. Gently simmer for 45 minutes. If the bones aren't yet clean, continue to simmer until they are—perhaps 5 or 10 more minutes. Strain the sauce and discard the solids. If you see fat on the surface, skim off most of it. Keep sauce warm.

To lard, or fill, the lamb loins: Chop very finely, by hand or in a food processor, the truffles, marjoram, and pancetta. (With a food processor —or a mortar—you can achieve the creamy filling shown on p. 104, but a very fine chop is OK, too.) Transfer to a bowl, add the extra-virgin olive oil, and stir gently to mix. Then, with your finger, make a tunnel through each loin and push the truffle filling into it. Dust each loin with flour. Heat a fry pan over high heat, and then add the remaining 5 tablespoons of olive oil, butter, and sage. Cook the loins to desired doneness, and then remove and keep warm. Discard the pan liquids, wipe the pan with a towel, add the sauce to the pan and heat it gently. To serve, slice each loin into 3 pieces and place the slices flat on a plate so that you can see the filling. Pour the warmed sauce over the lamb and place 4 potato halves on each plate. Serve immediately.

BROCCOLINI

Serves 4

Featured on p. 108

Like most side dishes at FARINA, this dish is simple by design—a counterpart to a more complex main dish such as lamb loins larded with black truffles. "Broccolini pairs best with wild things," says Paolo. Think truffles and mushrooms.

2 bunches broccolini

1 T coarse sea salt

2 T olive oil

1 clove garlic

pinch red chili flakes

Trim the bottoms of the broccolini stalks about 1 inch, as they can be woody. Bring a medium-sized pot of water to a boil and add the salt so that the water tastes, as they say in Genoa, "as salty as the sea." Cook the broccolini for 4 to 7 minutes, until just tender, then remove from the water and shake off excess.

Heat a sauté pan over medium heat and add the oil, garlic (smashed with your palm or fist so that it flavors the oil but doesn't dominate the dish), and broccolini. Add a pinch of chili flakes plus coarse sea salt to taste. Sauté the broccolini for 2 minutes to coat it with the garlic oil and give it a roasty flavor. Serve immediately.

SACRIPANTINA

Genovese Layer Cake | *Serves 8–10*

Featured on p. 110

Until about thirty years ago, pastry shops were common in Genoa. Today they're rare, mainly because desserts like sacripantina involve more labor than many shops want to invest. But the rarity of this cake makes it special, and the flavor makes it worth the effort. Tip: Toast the hazelnuts in a 350°F oven for five to eight minutes to enhance their flavor. Let them cool a bit, and then rub them briskly between your palms. "If you get eighty percent of the skins off this way, that's fine," says Paolo. To grind the hazelnuts, pulse them in a food processor, pound them in a mortar, or chop them.

Cake

5 large eggs

1/2 c sugar

4 T (1/2 stick) unsalted butter, melted and cooled slightly

1 c all-purpose flour

pinch fine sea salt

Buttercream Filling

1-1/4 c (2 1/2 sticks) unsalted butter, at room temperature

1 T maraschino liqueur (or other cherry-flavored liqueur)

1 3/4 c confectioners' sugar

3 large egg yolks

1/2 t vanilla extract

2 oz dark chocolate, melted, cooled slightly

1/2 c hazelnuts, toasted and finely ground

To make the cake: Heat oven to 350°F. Butter and flour a 9-inch round cake pan. In the bowl from your stand mixer, whisk together the eggs and sugar until combined, and then place the bowl just above a pan of simmering water. Continue to whisk about 2 minutes until sugar is dissolved and mixture is lukewarm. Then, using the mixer, whisk on medium-high for 5 to 10 minutes until the mixture is pale yellow and has reached the "ribbon stage." (Let some of it drip off the beaters; it should form a ribbon on the surface of the mixture.) Remove 1 cup of the egg mixture and add it to the melted butter; stir until combined. Set aside. In another bowl, sift flour with salt. Sift half of the flour mixture over the remaining egg mixture and gently fold until almost all of the flour is incorporated. Repeat with remaining flour mixture until all traces of flour have disappeared. Then gently fold in the egg-and-butter mixture. Spoon into the cake pan and bake for about 20 minutes until the cake is tan and bounces back when lightly pressed. Let cool on a rack for 10 minutes, then turn out on rack to cool completely.

To make the buttercream: In a mixer, combine the butter, liqueur, and sugar. Whisk at medium speed for 5 to 6 minutes until white, soft, and smooth. Turn mixer down to low and add egg yolks one at a time, beating well after each addition. Divide the buttercream evenly among three bowls. Into each of the bowls, stir in the vanilla extract, the chocolate, and the hazelnuts, respectively.

Line an 8-inch diameter bowl with plastic wrap. Slice the cake into 1/2-inch-wide strips. Line the bowl with one layer of cake slices, laid on their sides (cut surface exposed) and fitted snugly against each other. Spoon on the vanilla buttercream and smooth. Cover the vanilla buttercream with a layer of cake slices, followed by the chocolate buttercream. Add another layer of cake slices and top with the hazelnut buttercream. Finish with a layer of cake slices.

Cover the cake with plastic wrap and place another bowl on top to weigh it down. (Don't press down on the upper bowl; it's just there to help the cake set.) Refrigerate for 1 hour. To unmold the cake, invert the bowl and, if necessary, gently tug on the plastic wrap that lines the bowl. Slice and serve.

TORTINO DI CARCIOFI

Artichoke Frittata | *Serves 4*

Featured on p. 118

In this cross between a soufflé and frittata, lightness is key, and the key to lightness is to pop your ramekins into the oven just after you combine the ingredients. "Don't wait for the flour to settle," says Paolo. "Move quickly, no problem."

Fonduta Sauce

1/2 c heavy cream

2 oz fontina cheese, cubed

1 t finely chopped fresh marjoram

pinch of coarse sea salt

Tortino

4 medium or 6 small artichokes, about
 1-1/2 c when cleaned and sliced

2 T olive oil

1/4 c chopped white onion

1 clove garlic, smashed

1 t chopped fresh marjoram

1 t chopped flat-leaf parsley

sprinkle of coarse sea salt

1 T mascarpone cheese

2 T ricotta cheese

2 T grated Parmigiano-Reggiano cheese

2 large eggs, separated

2 T all-purpose flour

white or black truffle (optional)

Butter and flour four 6-ounce soufflé ramekins. Place in refrigerator to cool.

To make the fonduta sauce: In a double boiler, heat cream, fontina, marjoram, and a pinch of coarse sea salt. Stir constantly until the cheese has melted and the mixture is smooth. Turn off the heat and leave the sauce in the pot to stay warm until serving.

To make the tortino: Heat oven to 350°F. Wash the artichokes, pull off the tough outer leaves, halve lengthwise, and remove the chokes. Then thinly slice crosswise. Heat oil in a medium-sized fry pan. Add the artichokes, onion, garlic, herbs, and a sprinkle of coarse sea salt and sauté for 5 to 7 minutes until tender. Transfer to a bowl and stir in the cheeses and then the egg yolks. Beat egg whites until they form stiff peaks. Fold them in along with the flour, working gently to keep the mixture light and aerated. Fill ramekins 3/4 full and bake on a tray for 12 to 15 minutes until risen and golden.

To serve, you have a choice: Unmold each tortino by inverting it, gently, onto a plate. Then turn it right-side up and top with a few spoonfuls of fonduta sauce. Or serve each tortino in its ramekin and let your guests make holes in the centers to hold a bit of sauce. Either way, you can, if you wish, finish with a shaving of white or black truffle.

PANE DI CASTAGNE CON NOCI

Chestnut Bread with Walnuts | *Makes 2 loaves*

Featured on p. 124

In Liguria, abundant chestnuts make a warming, filling winter food. In this bread, they add a smoky note, balanced by the sweet of the walnuts. But go easy on the chestnut flour. It's not really flour at all, but ground nuts, strong in flavor and low in gluten, with no leavening action. Add too much and you'll get a pancake or a hockey puck.

1 t active dry yeast

3/4 c warm water

3 1/4 c starter (p. 173)

2 3/4 c unbleached bread flour

1/4 c chestnut flour

1 3/4 t coarse sea salt

1/4 c coarsely chopped walnuts

In a small bowl, dissolve yeast in water. Let sit 5 to 10 minutes until foamy. In the bowl of your stand mixer, combine the starter, flours, and yeast mixture. Using the dough hook, mix on low for 5 minutes and then check the consistency; it should be tacky but not sticky. If necessary, add a bit more water or flour. (Paolo likes our dough to be on the wet side because it makes the bread more chewy.) Then add the salt and walnuts and mix on medium speed for 3 minutes. Place the dough in a lightly oiled bowl, cover, and put aside in a warm place to rise for about 1 hour. The dough should double in size.

Turn the dough onto a floured work surface and divide it in half. Shape into rounds, cover, and let rest for 15 minutes. Then shape into 2 oblong loaves.

Place the loaves on a baking sheet, cover, and allow to rise for 45 minutes to 1 hour. Press the dough gently. If your fingerprint remains, the dough is ready for baking. If your fingerprint pops back quickly, wait a few more minutes.

Heat oven to 425°F. With a knife, make a cut about 1/2 inch deep lengthwise down the center of each loaf. (This enables the loaves to expand without cracking.) Place loaves in the oven and spritz with water to create the steam that makes a crunchy, shiny crust. Reduce heat to 400°F and bake for 25 minutes. Check sides and bottom; if not hard and dark tan, leave in oven for another 10 minutes, then check again. Transfer loaves to a rack to cool for 30 minutes before slicing.

TAGLIERINI AI VENTI ROSSI CON TRIFOLA BIANCA

Taglierini with White Truffles | *Serves 4*

Featured on p. 130

Paolo says that "if you want to please the white truffle, shave it over an egg, sunny side up." In this traditional dish, he brings the truffle-and-egg pairing to pasta. Venti rossi *means "20 red," with the "red" being egg yolks. The actual number of yolks in the flour—17, 18, 20—is not as important as the consistency of the dough. It should be on the dry side, but not too dry. "If you cup some dough in your hands and it crumbles and falls apart, add another yolk," says Paolo.*

3 c Caputo brand "00" flour (or all-purpose flour)

17 to 19 large egg yolks

1-1/2 T coarse sea salt

4 T (1/2 stick) unsalted butter, softened

4 large egg yolks, for serving

pinch fine sea salt

.8-.9 oz (25 grams) fresh truffles, preferably white

Mound the flour on a cutting board or counter and make a deep well in the center. Pour 17 egg yolks into the well and beat them lightly with a fork for 20 seconds. Then gradually push dry flour into the well, stirring in a circular motion with your fingers, until you have a single ball of dough. Press your thumb into the ball. If the dough sticks to your thumb, add a bit more flour. When your thumb comes away clean, the dough is ready to knead. Knead dough for 2 to 3 minutes until smooth.

Divide the dough in half and then feed each piece into a pasta machine, starting on the widest setting. Pass each piece through 4 times, then move the roller to the next narrower notch and pass the dough through twice. Continue two passes on each successive notch until the dough is about as thick as a lasagna noodle.

Lay the pasta sheets on a floured work surface and cut into 1-foot lengths. Let the pasta sheets hang for 20 minutes to dry, or lay them out flat for 20 minutes on each side. (The drying helps the pasta strands pass cleanly through the taglierini cutter.) Using the taglierini attachment, run each pasta sheet through the pasta machine. Toss the resulting noodles in a bit of flour to keep them from sticking together.

Fill a large pot with water and place it over high heat to boil. As the water warms, stir in the salt. Gently stir the noodles into the boiling water and cook until *al dente*, testing after 2 minutes. Drain.

While the pasta cooks, melt the butter over medium heat in a sauté pan large enough to hold all of the pasta. Add the drained pasta to the pan and stir to coat with butter. Add a pinch of fine sea salt.

To serve, divide the pasta among 4 bowls. Make a well in the center of the pasta in each bowl. Place one egg yolk in each well, then shave some truffle over the top (shave white truffle with a truffle shaver; shave black truffle with a truffle shaver or a grater). Serve immediately.

FILETTO DI FASSONE CON PORCINI E SALSA AL BAROLO

Filet Mignon with Porcini and Barolo Sauce | *Serves 4*

Featured on p. 136

Nearly every restaurant in Genoa serves filet mignon in the wintertime, says Paolo, but many cooks add red wine to this dish too late in the process. "They reduce it too quickly. Minute-cooked wine is burnt wine. It's not true wine sauce." The moral of this story: Be patient with your sauce. Slow cooking will preserve more of the wine's character and nuance.

- 9 T olive oil, divided
- 3 T unsalted butter, divided
- 1/2 medium onion, 1 medium carrot, 1 stalk celery, roughly chopped
- 1 clove garlic, smashed
- 3 sprigs each thyme and rosemary
- 3 sage leaves
- 2 bay leaves
- 10 juniper berries
- 2 cloves
- 1/2 lb each beef bones and beef scraps (filet scraps or cheap cuts)
- 1-1/2 t coarse sea salt, divided
- 1 T all-purpose flour, plus more for dusting
- 2 c Barolo or Barbaresco (or other full-bodied red wine)
- 4 filets mignon of very similar size and weight (about 4 to 6 oz each)
- 14 oz porcini mushrooms
- 1/2 t chopped garlic
- 2 t chopped flat-leaf parsley
- 4 sage leaves

To make the sauce: Heat oven to 350°F. Place a medium roasting pan on the stovetop over high heat. Add 4 tablespoons olive oil and 1 tablespoon butter. Add the onion, carrot, celery, garlic clove, thyme, rosemary, sage, bay leaves, juniper berries, cloves, bones, scraps, and salt. Cook, stirring frequently, for 4 minutes. Sprinkle on 1 tablespoon of flour, stir, and place the pan in the oven for 10 minutes. Remove the pan from the oven, stir in the wine, and cook on the stovetop over high heat for 2 minutes. Stir in 1 cup water. Place pan back in the oven and reduce the temperature to 325°F. Cook for 1-1/2 hours. Strain the sauce into a pot. Season with coarse sea salt to taste. Then "shock" the sauce by submerging most of the pot in a bowl of ice water for about 12 minutes until cool. This step stops the cooking and preserves the flavor and integrity of the sauce. Set the sauce aside. (If it will be more than 30 minutes before you serve, cover and refrigerate.)

Remove filets from refrigerator about 30 minutes before cooking.

To prepare the mushrooms: Gently remove any dirt with a damp towel. Slice mushrooms about 1/4 inch thick. Heat a sauté pan over medium heat, add 2 tablespoons olive oil and then the mushrooms, plus 1/2 teaspoon coarse sea salt. Sauté lightly for 3 minutes. Then add chopped garlic and parsley and cook for about 2 more minutes until mushrooms are brown and tender. Let rest, off heat.

To cook the filets: Heat oven to 350°F. Lightly season each filet with coarse sea salt and then dust with flour on all sides. Over high heat, place an ovenproof fry pan or sauté pan large enough to hold all 4 filets without them touching. When the pan is hot, add 3 tablespoons olive oil. Add the filets to the hot oil and cook 2 minutes on each side to get a good sear. Take another 30 seconds to sear the edges, too. Then add 2 tablespoons butter and the sage leaves to the pan. Turn and bathe the filets in the butter and sage. Make sure the filets are not touching each other, and then place them in the oven. For rare, cook 5 minutes. For medium-rare, 7 minutes. For medium, 10 minutes. (Your cooking times may vary, as ovens vary.)

Remove filets from the pan and let them rest, uncovered, for about 4 minutes to assure the juices won't rush out at the first cut. While the meat rests, heat the sauce gently until just warm. Check sauce for seasoning. To serve, place each filet on a plate. Spoon a few tablespoons of sauce over each filet, then serve the mushrooms alongside. Serve immediately.

PATATE NOVELLE ARROSTO

Roasted Potatoes | *Serves 4*

Featured on p. 142

Good potatoes don't need much manipulation. They just need a hot oven, a generous hand with fresh herbs, and the benediction of olive oil and butter. "Express the potato!" says Paolo. "Celebrate it!"

- 9 fingerling potatoes (or other small, waxy potatoes, such as red)
- 3 T olive oil
- 1 t chopped fresh rosemary
- 1 t chopped fresh sage
- 1 t chopped flat-leaf parsley
- 1 t chopped fresh thyme
- generous pinch coarse sea salt
- 2 T unsalted butter

Heat oven to 400°F. Wash potatoes. Cut them in half lengthwise. Toss in a bowl with the oil, herbs, and salt. Melt the butter on the stove in an ovenproof pan, add the potatoes and herbs, and stir to coat. Place potatoes in the oven. Check them after 25 minutes. They should be crisp and dark tan and cooked all the way through.

CREMINO D'ALBA

Custard with Caramel | *Serves 4*

Featured on p. 144

Paolo first made this dessert nearly 30 years ago when he was a prep cook at Aladino restaurant in Genoa. With its heavy cream, cremino *is made for winter, but it's also paradoxically light and refreshing, similar to panna cotta. Note: Paolo uses sheets of fish gelatin in this recipe. If you can find them, use them.*

Caramel

1/2 c sugar

Cremino

1-1/2 c heavy cream

1-1/2 t powdered gelatin

1-1/2-inch long by 1/2-inch wide piece of orange peel, bitter pith removed

1/2 vanilla bean, split lengthwise (or 1/2 t vanilla extract)

3 T sugar

2 t Grand Marnier

3 large egg yolks, at room temperature

To make the caramel: Bring sugar and 3 tablespoons of water to boil in a small saucepan over medium-low heat, Cook without stirring until the sugar browns lightly, or caramelizes. Then stir gently until the caramel is a thick syrup and dark golden brown. Divide the caramel among four 4-ounce ramekins and set aside.

To make the cremino: Put 1/2 cup cream in a wide bowl and sprinkle the gelatin evenly over the top. Let sit for 10 minutes to soften. In a small saucepan, gently heat the remaining 1 cup cream along with the orange peel, vanilla, sugar, and Grand Marnier until the mixture reaches a low simmer. Add the gelatin mixture and whisk well for 3 to 5 minutes until smooth. Take care not to let the mixture come to a full boil.

In a separate bowl, whisk the egg yolks. Add a bit of the heated cream mixture to the yolks, whisking all the while. Add the remaining cream mixture one-third at a time, whisking continuously. Incorporating the heated cream slowly will help ensure that the egg yolks don't scramble. Strain to remove the orange peel, vanilla bean (if using), and any lumps.

Pour the custard into the ramekins and refrigerate for at least 6 hours to set. (The cremino will keep up to 7 days in the refrigerator.) To serve, invert each ramekin onto a dessert plate. If the cremino won't release, dip the base of the ramekin in warm water to gently loosen the caramel.

Note: At the restaurant, Paolo tops the cremino with shards of hazelnut brittle. To make the brittle, combine 1/2 cup sugar, 1/4 cup water, and 1/4 teaspoon lemon juice in a small saucepan. Stir over medium-low heat until sugar dissolves. Increase heat and boil, swirling the pan occasionally, until the syrup turns a deep golden brown. Remove from heat and place base of saucepan in a bowl of ice water to stop the cooking, swirling pan occasionally for about 7 or 8 minutes. Add 1/4 cup toasted, chopped hazelnuts and stir to blend. Pour mixture onto a baking sheet lined with a silicone mat or parchment. Cool until firm. Break the brittle into large pieces.

BASIC PASTA DOUGH

With all due respect to dry pasta, good handmade pasta has a certain lightness and freshness and delicacy about it. And it absorbs sauces beautifully. In this recipe, the white wine adds silkiness and the cheese adds chew. If you can't find finely ground doppio zero *pasta flour from Molino Caputo of Naples, Italy, use all-purpose flour. Just make sure your flour is as fresh as it can be. Your eggs, too. They'll reward you with better texture and flavor.*

2 c Caputo brand "00" flour (or all-purpose flour)
2 large eggs, at room temperature
1/4 cup dry white wine
1 T finely grated Parmigiano-Reggiano cheese

Mound the flour on a cutting board or counter and make a deep well in the center. Crack the eggs into the well and beat them lightly with a fork for 20 seconds. Add the wine and cheese to the well. Then gradually push dry flour into the well, stirring in a circular motion with your fingers, until you have a single ball of dough. Press your thumb into the ball. If the dough sticks to your thumb, add a bit more flour. When your thumb comes away clean, the dough is ready to knead. Knead dough for 7 to 9 minutes until smooth. If you don't use the dough immediately, cover it with a damp cloth. You can also wrap the dough in plastic wrap and refrigerate it for up to 3 days. Just be sure to remove it from the refrigerator an hour before using to warm it up and make it pliable enough to work with.

BASICS

STARTER FOR BREAD RECIPES

Starter is the beginning of bread. It bubbles and smells and looks alive. If you want your bread on the mild side, let the starter sit and ferment for five hours. If you want your bread on the sour side, wait eight hours.

heaping 1/4 t active dry yeast
1/2 cup warm water
2 1/2 c unbleached bread flour
1 c water, at room temperature

In a small bowl, dissolve the yeast in the warm water and let it sit for 5 to 10 minutes until foamy. Then combine it with the flour and water in a mixing bowl. The mixture should look wet and sticky like pancake batter. Cover the bowl with plastic wrap and let it sit for 6 hours until the starter bubbles and smells yeasty. Then use immediately or refrigerate, covered, for up to 3 days. Remove from the refrigerator at least 1 hour before using, to take the chill off.

THE ARCHITECTURE OF FARINA: OLD WORLD NEW

FARINA design is a lot like FARINA cooking: It's simple but not easy. How, after all, to create a restaurant space that honors both Italy and California, the old and the new?

Enter Brett Terpeluk. He's an American but he speaks Italian, is married to Italian landscape architect Monica Viarengo, spent ten years working with celebrated Italian architect Renzo Piano, and, when he's not working in the San Francisco office of his Studio Terpeluk design firm, he works in its Genoa office.

For restaurant FARINA, Brett and Monica created a delicate balance: The room is airy but the feeling is intimate. The look is modern but most materials are old.

Brett's design began on his sketchpad, but it really got started in a salvage yard on the outskirts of Genoa. There, Brett and Monica discovered a trove of antique sinks and drainboards carved by hand out of Carrara marble. These pieces, combined, are more than mere counters at FARINA; they're touchstones that embody three tons of tradition.

Once he established pale gray marble as his baseline color, Brett warmed the room with touches of red in chairs and stools, and with light-brown benches, tables, credenza, and wine rack, all built of guanacaste wood reclaimed from a river bottom in Costa Rica.

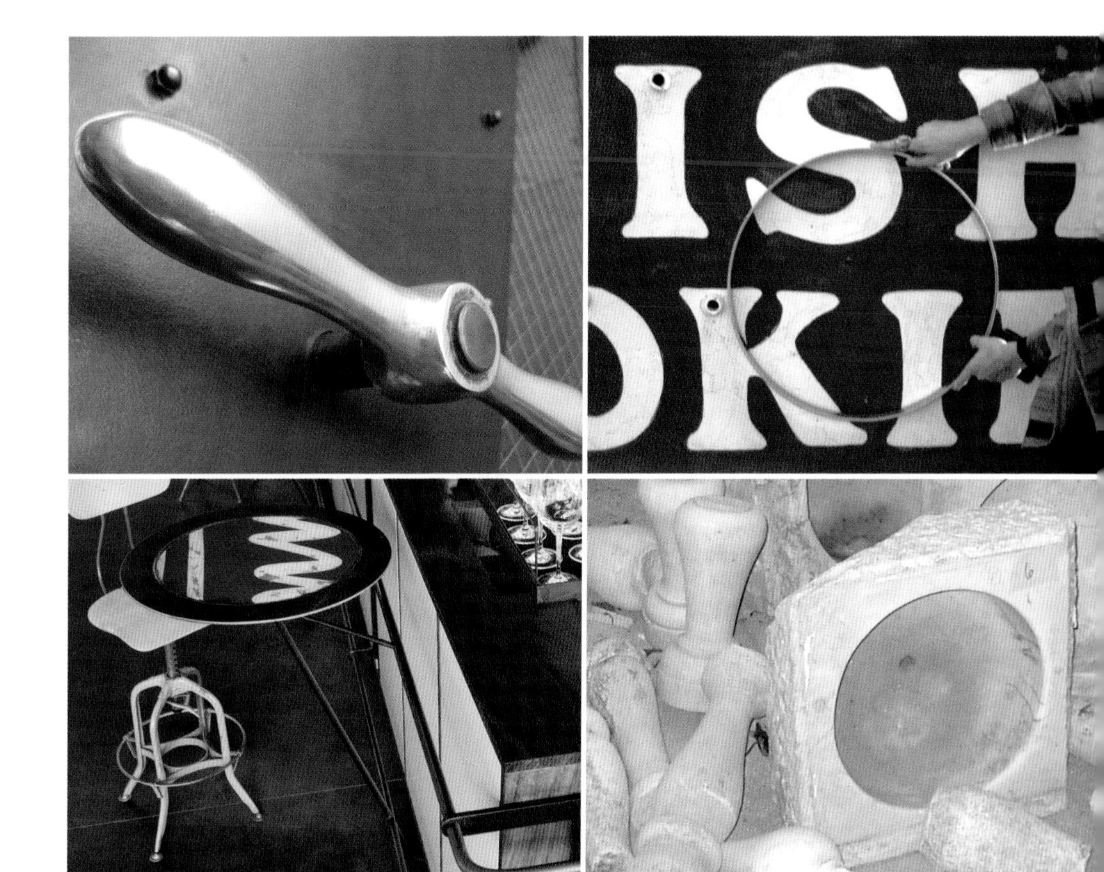

The gray concrete floor, curved concrete bench seat, and black steel shelving add heft and a sense of permanence. The pale walls, white-painted rafters, aluminum chairs, and chrome-and-glass sconces brighten the space and add industrial shimmer.

Just as the past informs FARINA's recipes, the past speaks in its furnishings. In this building that once housed a cookie factory, the original dough-mixing paddles now serve as handles on the front door. The midcentury red-and-white "Anna's Danish Cookies" sign was laser-cut into round tabletops. Old schoolhouse chairs, rescued from a Northern California salvage yard, flank the long central dining table at which large groups gather and where, if the space is free, the FARINA staff—cooks, servers, bartenders, dishwashers—converges for "family meal."

By day, FARINA bathes in sunlight. By night, it glows by the light of red octopus chandeliers. The front wall of windows, inset from the building face, enables outdoor seating just off the sidewalk and inside the property line. On warm autumn evenings, these tables fill fast.

Upstairs on the roof terrace, Monica created a garden that is not only beautiful but productive: Guests enjoy the MaestraPeace mural on The Women's Building across the street, and cooks often pop upstairs to snip fresh herbs.

All told, the idea is to create an aura of welcome. At FARINA, every element—from the custom-built furnishings to the plates made to order by a local pottery—serves to soothe the eye, to enhance each meal, to honor the love and care that the cooks pour into every dish.

FAR LEFT: Steel rails protect the central island and provide a footrest, too. LEFT: Antique marble sinks and drainboards, shipped from a salvage yard in Genoa, gain a new purpose in the New World. ABOVE: Octopus chandeliers float in an oxygen sea. RIGHT: The custom-built wine rack, crafted of guanacaste wood plucked from a river bottom in Costa Rica, adds efficient storage and visual warmth.

THE ROOF GARDEN: NEW WORLD NEWER

If the first floor of restaurant FARINA subtly favors the Old World, the second level celebrates the New. Here you'll find a 2,000-square-foot roof garden that's designed to feel fresh, airy, and quintessentially California. Then again, it might be a small slice of heaven.

The celestial theme begins with variations on the color blue, which appears across the street in the MaestraPeace mural, in glazed garden pots, in a row of acoustic panels, and most strikingly in the swath of blue sky above the center of the garden. Unimpeded by awnings, the light from this sky nourishes a living landscape of succulents and flowering vines.

For furnishings, the rooftop contains the same ingredients —marble, steel, and wood—as the main dining room downstairs, but here the ratio shifts. In contrast to the massive marble counters in their antique Italian majesty, up here the marble is new and especially pale, and it appears only in tabletops shaped to look buoyant and almost birdlike. Underfoot, off-white pavers reinforce the impression of lightness.

Along the edge of the terrace, a slender steel pergola supports gray awnings that shelter each table. Cypress slab benches, custom built from reclaimed Northern California lumber, are suspended by the structure as if to float, imparting a sense of flight. The benches form booths to create private "rooms," with pendant lamps and warming heaters adding their soft glow to the night sky.

The roof terrace adjoins an intimate private dining room and grappa bar, lined with blue leather booths and steel-and-marble tables. This room can be reserved or opened to the garden, inviting a flow between indoors and out.

With this rooftop garden, FARINA has taken a bold step skyward on a journey that, in a way, resembles *The Divine Comedy* by Dante Alighieri. You begin downstairs in the kitchen, or the Inferno. You cross the gray industrial concrete floors of the main dining room and begin climbing the Purgatory of corkscrew stairs that carry you upward on a blind and mysterious path. At the top of the stairs, you discover a garden oasis where friends and family, food and drink await. Is this Paradise?

ABOVE: Succulents form a living landscape on the center of the roof terrace, while wooden benches form booths along the edge. The blue acoustic panels behind the benches do more than damp noise; they echo the sky overhead. ABOVE RIGHT: Marble slab tables, gently pointed on one side, escape the dull tyranny of the rectangle—and seem poised to take flight. Stainless steel cables help secure the blackened steel pergola and also divide the booths so that each feels like a private room. BELOW RIGHT: When viewed from the side, these cypress slab benches appear to hover.

LEFT: Vladas Girininkas, the perfectionist. ABOVE: Roberto Merlo, the flying photographer. BELOW LEFT: Angela DeCenzo, tattooed flower child. BELOW: Norma Cordova, seeker of beauty. FAR RIGHT: Norma and Angela celebrate completion of this book.

FARINA PHOTOGRAPHY: IT TAKES A TEAM

We never planned to take photographs of our dishes, much less build a whole book around them. But, as with many things FARINA, the story of our photographs is a journey of serendipity.

The journey began five years ago when we arranged to take two of FARINA's American-born cooks to Italy so they could visit the birthplace of our cuisine. But there was one problem: Paolo's sous chef reported that the cooks' tour would collide with his girlfriend's birthday.

Well, what better birthday gift than a trip to Italy? So Angela DeCenzo joined us. Only at the end of the trip did she mention that she was a photographer. A few months later, we asked her if she would help us celebrate the season's first white truffles by photographing them. She and her photography partner, Norma Cordova, responded with shots so vivid that they looked good enough to eat. For the first time in photographs, we could see and sense truffles in all their lumpy, smelly glory.

That's how Angela and Norma came to photograph the ingredients, the dishes, the landscapes, and the people in these pages. Together, Angela, born to hippie parents and raised in a Volkswagen bus on a tour of America, and Norma, a wild child running free through Oregon apple orchards, contribute to this book a childlike wonder and a strong love of nature.

When it came time to photograph the architectural and culinary design of restaurant FARINA, fate brought us to Vladas Girininkas, a Lithuanian fanatic for photography. Vladas sees the world through his lenses, has an uncanny radar for camera shops, and, with only the slightest provocation, will tell you all about cameras and equipment and photographic methods. You'd never know that he is usually quiet and shy, and it makes no difference if you don't understand Lithuanian. In the studio or on location, Vladas's wife, Gražina, acts as his artistic eye, directing him to see lines, shapes, colors, and elegance. Together, Vladas and Gražina bring to style and design details the same passion that Michelangelo brought to slabs of marble.

Finally, to convey a true sense of Liguria, the land between sea and sky, we needed to free ourselves of gravity. So we sought out Roberto Merlo, an Italian photographer whose photographic partner is a helicopter. Roberto has created thousands of airborne photographs of Italy in general and Liguria in particular. He says that from above, Liguria looks pure and wild, but he also acknowledges that "the deeper soul of Liguria has been carved by the hands of its inhabitants."

Roberto is widely known as "the flying photographer," but he thinks of himself as a fisherman who, from the privileged observatory of the sky, catches the best of life. In these pages, he shows Liguria from the perspective of a seabird—or an angel.

Each of these photographers created images that do more than depict the making of a Ligurian dish or the design of an Italian restaurant. They capture the essence of FARINA.

龍

FRIENDS, FAMILY, FUTURE

The story of FARINA is the story of people bound by a passion for the foods and the life that we cherish. On these two pages we picture Italian locals whose enthusiasm inspires us, and below, in roughly chronological order, we name ten friends who have played key roles in our development.

As usual, we begin in Genoa, and we begin with Simone Laboa. Simone is the son of Paolo, our founding chef in San Francisco. When we first invited Paolo to join us, he hesitated. He didn't know English and he'd never been to America. But eight-year-old Simone said, "Dad, why not?"

James H. Kostelni, our first true friend in America, managed the construction of restaurant FARINA, building bridges between architects, contractors, and San Francisco city officials. He also shipped, by next-day air, an elevator from Germany—six months before we needed it. That's why we call him our "mess maker."

Giulio Viarengo paced the floor of FARINA as our commodore of service. With his impeccable suits and his eye for every detail, he inspired all of us to aim high.

Angelo and Yvonne Sangiacomo, San Francisco icons with Ligurian roots, booked the restaurant while FARINA was still under construction, inviting 100 friends and family members to opening night on June 5, 2007.

Roberto Marcialis, back in Genoa, engineered our budget and gave us sage advice and an upbeat spirit in times of doubt and difficulty. Also, he always stood ready to fly to San Francisco for a FARINA meal.

Brendan McKenna conceived and designed this book to express the FARINA aesthetic—and to celebrate la dolce vita.

Evan Elliot turned hazy ideas into edible sentences. He gave voice to our vision.

Lisa Elliot fine-tuned our design, kept us on schedule despite strong resistance, and prepared this book for printing.

Special mention to Amado Garrone, the baby in the picture, who played with a pile of farina. In so doing, he embodied the innocence and purity that we strive to emulate.

Beyond these ten special friends, we acknowledge everyone on team FARINA, past and present. We offer our deepest gratitude to everyone in the back of the house, the front of the house, the maintenance crew, the valet parking team, the managers, and our office group.

Special thanks to the farmers, fishers, and foragers who supply us with such wonderful ingredients, to the city of San Francisco for its cosmopolitan air, and to those food critics who understand and appreciate our mission.

Thanks also to our families, who taught us to act with integrity, and to our friends, who encouraged us to pursue our dreams. Their support sustains us.

This book is a toast to our five-year anniversary, but it's not a mark of completion. We seek, now, to not only maintain our standards but to reach ever higher. We'll expand our offerings to embrace all of Italy. We also plan to open in more locations and to make more room at our table, so that wherever your travels take you, when you find a FARINA, you can sit down, take a breath, savor your meal, and celebrate life.

Luca Minna and Laura Garrone

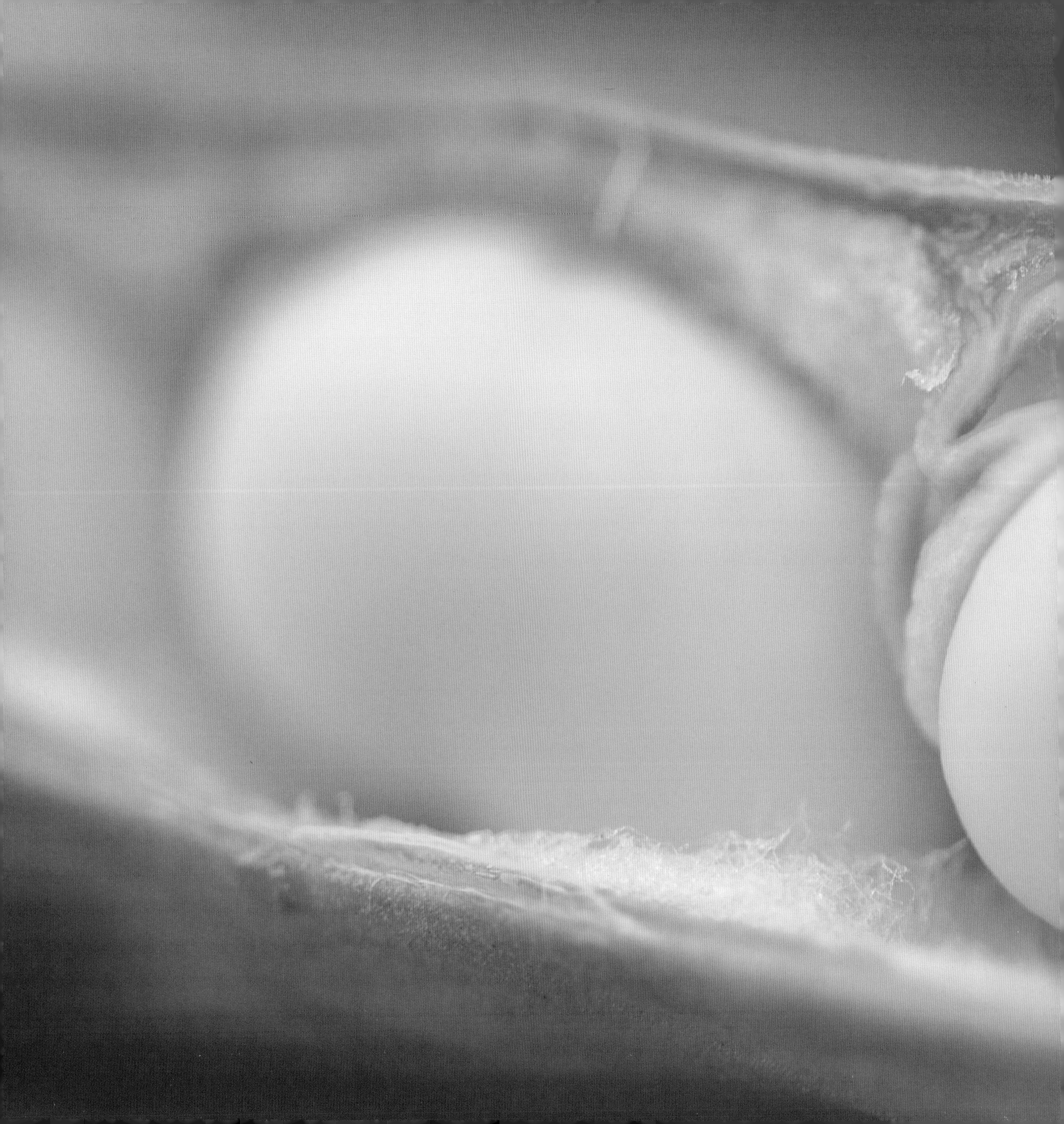

Manufactured in China.

M3 Media Group
700 Valencia Street, Suite 9
San Francisco, CA 94110
415 864 4033
www.m3media-group.com